History of France

A Captivating Guide to French History

.

Free Bonus from Captivating History
(Available for a Limited time)

Hi History Lovers!

Now you have a chance to join our exclusive history list so you can get your first history ebook for free as well as discounts and a potential to get more history books for free! Simply visit the link below to join.

Captivatinghistory.com/ebook

Also, make sure to follow us on Facebook, Twitter and Youtube by searching for Captivating History.

Contents

Introduction – Let's Go to Lascaux!

In September of 1940, two months after France fell to Hitler, a group of teenagers was out walking in the woods near the village of Montignac in the Dordogne region of southwestern France. The story goes that the boys were out looking for reported buried treasure at the end of an underground tunnel somewhere in the area. The legend had been going around for years, but this group of boys was sure they were onto something when they (or their dog, in one version) found a large hole in the ground.

The boys gathered around the hole, dropping rocks into it to get an idea of how deep it might be. Thinking it wasn't all that deep, they made their way one by one down a narrow shaft that went down about fifty feet. When they got to the bottom, they found themselves in a dimly lit cave covered with an amazing assortment of paintings. The boys weren't sure exactly what they were looking at, but they were pretty sure it was unique. After going promising each other to keep their findings a secret, they went back the next day and then decided they could make money off of what they had found. They decided to charge admission to some of their local friends and acquaintances.

Word spread, and hundreds of locals came to see the paintings, each with a theory about what they were and how they got there. Word finally got to a member of a local prehistory society whose members collected fossils and examined caves in the area. When he went down the hole, he felt sure he was looking at prehistoric paintings and instructed the boys to not let anyone else in until he could notify a local expert. This is the story behind the discovery of the amazing cave paintings of Lascaux.

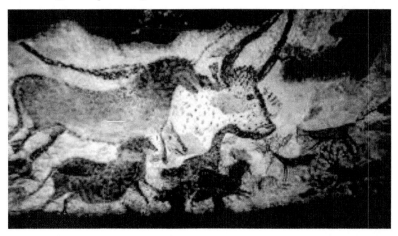

Illustration 1: One small sample of the Lascaux cave paintings.

The Lascaux paintings are estimated to be between 15,000 to 17,000 years old. Today, only recognized experts can go into the original cave to study the paintings. The climate is very carefully controlled because in the years after their discovery, thousands of people went to see the paintings, some even touching them. Others faded due to the amount of condensation and carbon dioxide caused by the visitors' breathing. The caves were closed to the public in 1963. In 2016, an amazing reconstruction of the paintings was created in a site nearby.

Were the inhabitants of the Lascaux caves "French"? Of course not. But the paintings at Lascaux and elsewhere in France prove that the land we call France has had a long history of human habitation going back thousands of years. It also appears those residents have had the same taste for art and culture that the people of France have always been noted for. Captivating History's *History of France* will introduce you to one of the most fascinating and influential nations in the world. French history is so involved and so intricate that it would (and has) taken forests to provide the paper to write it all on. For this book, we're going to introduce you to some of the greatest Frenchmen and women in history, and while you're getting to know them, we hope you get a feeling for the time and events that they lived in or perhaps even created themselves.

Chapter 1 – Just the Facts

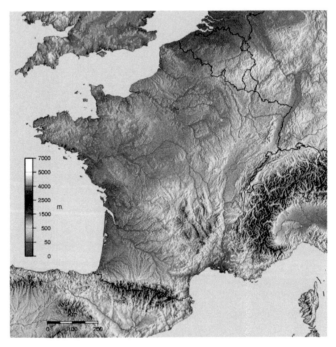

Modern France and the American state of Texas are about the same size (France is 248,573 mi², while Texas is 268,597 mi²). That gives you an idea of the size of the United States as a whole compared to the largest country in Europe, discounting, as some do, Russia and Ukraine.

France has been both blessed and cursed by its location and topography. As you can see from the topographical map above, France is surrounded by water on three sides: the North Sea/English Channel on the northern coast, the Atlantic Ocean to the west, and the Mediterranean Sea to the south. These bodies of water provide great riches in terms of fish and other resources, and they have allowed France to establish seaborne trade throughout its history. These waterways have also allowed the country to project power not only in Europe but also around the world. This has been a great blessing, as they have allowed France to become one of the richest and most powerful countries in the world.

Unfortunately for the French, those waterways also expose the nation to invaders from overseas, though, in one case in 1944, the invasion from overseas was welcomed. Most notably, France's long English Channel coast exposes it to the country that had been its mortal enemy for centuries: England/Great Britain. However, times change, and France and England are close allies today.

In the Middle Ages, France's long coastlines exposed it to the ravages of the Vikings. This was made worse by the incredible number of navigable rivers that flow through France. The most famous French river, the Seine, flows from the English Channel directly to and through Paris—a fact discovered early on by the Norse invaders. The Seine, other large rivers (such as the Loire), and their many branches allowed the Vikings easy and rapid access to the interior of the country.

The rivers of France are also a blessing. They bring water deep into the heart of the country, and before the advent of trucks, cars, and planes, they were the primary economic highways of the country, bringing goods from one area to another. As you can see by the large amounts of green on the map, France is an incredibly fertile country, growing not only abundant crops but, as any chef will tell you, also some of the best natural ingredients in the world.

Another mixed blessing is France's location vis-à-vis the other nations of western Europe. We've already mentioned England, with whom France has gone to war countless times over the centuries. Today, France borders eight countries, though, at other times in history, French territory was either larger or smaller, as was the number of bordering nations. Three of those countries are quite small: Luxembourg, Andorra, and Monaco. The other five are Belgium, Italy, Spain, Switzerland, and Germany. Germany, which has only been a united nation state since 1871, has been a thorn in the side of France (to put it *very* mildly) since its inception, though at times, various German states (mostly on the French border) aligned themselves with France.

Since the French Revolution and the rise of Napoleon Bonaparte, the French and the Germans (before the Germans unified into the large and powerful state of Prussia) have fought four or five major wars, depending on how you divide historical eras. Between 1789 and 1815, the French and many of the German principalities fought a series of conflicts that saw France overrun virtually all of modern-day Germany. From 1870 to 1871, the Germans, under Prussian leadership, invaded France as part of their plan to unite all the German-speaking peoples into one nation. The Franco-Prussian War was a disaster for France. Some forty years later, World War I began, and the Germans invaded France yet again, conquering and occupying its richest regions for four years but never subduing the French nation. In 1940, the Germans under Hitler conquered France and subjected her to brutal occupation for four years. Today, France and Germany, thankfully, are among the closest allies on the planet.

France was the most populous nation in Europe up to the time of Napoleon and a bit beyond, which, combined with other factors, gave it great strength. Today, the population of France is just under sixty-eight million people, a number that has held steady for about a century.

The majority of the population is ethnically French, although there are sizable ethnically German populations in its east. Since the end of the French colonial period (circa 1945–1961), the nation has seen an influx of immigrants from former French colonies in Southeast Asia, Africa, and the Middle East. Some 7 to 9 percent of the population is Muslim, which, in recent years, has become a national issue. Some argue for limits on immigration even though generations of French Muslims are native-born, and others argue that the French are prejudiced against foreigners and, in particular, Muslims.

France has been and still is overwhelmingly Roman Catholic, though the number of people calling themselves "non-believers" has grown since the late 19th century. A small but culturally significant population of French Jews and Buddhists lives throughout the country, mostly in the larger cities, and most of the country's population as a whole is urban (around 81 percent).

France has one of the largest gross domestic product (GDP) in the world at nearly three trillion US dollars. Tourism brings in a large amount of money, as France is the most visited country in the world. The GDP of Russia, which is many times the size of France, is just over half of that amount, which speaks to both political history and stability as well as geography.

France's main trading partners are Germany, Belgium, Spain, the United Kingdom, Italy, the Netherlands, China, and the United States.

France produces most of the agriculture needed to support its population and exports its agricultural products throughout the world. Natural resources are abundant, especially in the northeast. Coal, iron, bauxite, zinc, gypsum, timber, and fish are among its most plentiful resources. One thing that France lacks in abundance is petroleum, which is one reason why the nation has become highly involved (along with its allies) in the Middle East.

France is not the military superpower it once was, but it is part of NATO (the North Atlantic Treaty Organization), which was created as an alliance against the communist Soviet Union after WWII. Today, NATO includes not only most of the western European nations but also a considerable number of eastern European nations, with the unsaid uniting fact being a continued suspicion and fear of Russia and its leadership.

France is one of a handful of nations that possesses nuclear weapons, and its arsenal alone is likely enough to destroy the planet. Its navy and air force are powerful enough to exert France's influence throughout the world, and its military has been and is still involved in many of the world's hotspots. The Middle East and Central Africa, in particular, are two areas in which France had considerable colonial possessions.

France's government is headed by a president, though officially, the position is labeled as the chief of state. The prime minister acts as the head of government (an important but largely ceremonial post). The legislature consists of two houses: the Sénat (Senate) and the Assemblée Nationale (National Assembly), which functions similarly to the United States Senate and House of Representatives. France's national judiciary consists of a large number of judges divided into sections and assignments.

Lastly, though French is the primary language of the nation, a sizable portion of the population speaks French as well as another language or regional dialect. Provencal, Breton, Alsatian/German, Basque, and Arabic are the major language groupings, along with a sizable number of Vietnamese and Spanish/Catalan speakers in the south as well. A significant portion of the population speaks English as a second language, though the journey from French being the language of diplomacy and business to English has not been an easy one, as many English-speaking tourists know!

Illustration 2: Names in bold are the eighteen regions of France and its major cities.

Chapter 2 – From the Last Great Ice Age to the Rise of Rome

Prior to the Great Ice Age (beginning about 30,000 years ago and ending about 10,000 years ago), our evolutionary ancestors had moved from eastern Africa into the Middle East and wandered off on four main routes to populate the "Old World." One branch slowly made its way into Asia, another into the steppes of today's Russia and central Asia, one into western Africa, and another into Europe.

Anthropologists believe that the most famous groups of the advanced primate family, Neanderthals and the Cro-Magnon people, reached as far north as modern-day Denmark and Great Britain, which was connected to Europe at the time by an expanse of land known today as Doggerland.

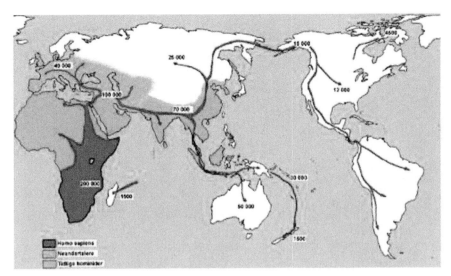

Illustration 3: Early human migration, including the later migrations into the Pacific and the Americas. (Courtesy Khan Academy)

Then, with the spreading of the glacial ice, which made most of Europe uninhabitable, our ancestors retreated southward. It's believed that two main areas of habitable land remained in Eurasia: one in the area of modern Ukraine and the other in the borderlands of today's France and Spain. When the weather began to get warmer about 10,000 years ago, our ancestors, both Neanderthals and *Homo sapiens*, moved slowly back into the spaces vacated by the ice.

One of the groups that remained in what is called the "Franco-Cantabrian refugium" (Cantabria being a region of northern Spain), which sheltered our ancestors, were the direct ancestors of today's Basque people, whose language, *Euskara*, is both the oldest and most unique of the European languages. (Actually, most linguists believe that *Euskara* is unrelated to any other European language.)

Over the next 8,000 years, a succession of cultures developed and faded into history in many of the areas of western Europe, including France. Today, these cultural groups are known by the characteristics of their art, tools, and other implements (such as urns, pitchers, etc.)

From about 3100 BCE to around 2350 BCE, the culture known today as the Corded Ware culture populated northern France, southern Scandinavia, southern Germany, and today's Russia. As you can see in the picture below, their pottery shows rough "cords" in their construction and outer design.

Illustration 4: Examples of Corded Ware pottery in the Berlin Prehistory Museum dating from circa 2500 BCE.

The peoples of the Corded Ware culture were centered in northwestern Europe and eastward. Toward the end of this cultural period, another group of prehistoric humans, known today as the Bell Beaker culture (named, yet again, for the characteristics of their art and implements), expanded from today's France and Spain and into other parts of Europe. This occurred in roughly 2400 BCE. Generally speaking, the Bell Beaker culture was the last of the Stone Age cultures, for it was followed by what is known as the Atlantic Bronze and Nordic Bronze Ages, which had many commonalities and significant differences as well.

*Illustration 5: Example of Bell Beaker
pottery—note the bell-like shape.*

The peoples of today's France, Spain, Switzerland, Italy, Great Britain, Ireland, and Denmark developed the use of bronze in c. 1700 BCE, and they also developed their own cultures with significant trade routes and an advanced economy. At about the same time, the peoples of Scandinavia moved into their own separate bronze age, the so-called Nordic Bronze Age, which developed unique artistic and societal differences from the rest of Europe.

Atlantic Bronze Age exchange products:
Imports: *Exports:*
   • Urnfields' crested helmets   • Tube sickles (Britain)
   • "Elbow" fibulae   • Tube and double ring axes
   "Cleavage" shields   (Portugal)

   ➤➤ Approx. western limit of Urnfields expansion

*Illustration 6: Significant archaeological finds
of the Atlantic Bronze Age.*

Take a good look at the map above. Generally speaking, the extent of the development of the Atlantic Bronze Age indicates the spread of the Celtic peoples, of whom the Gauls were a part. The Gauls and Celts inhabited large parts of central Europe in the time before the rise of Rome. Our story of France begins with the many Gallic tribes of France as the Roman Empire spread into western Europe.

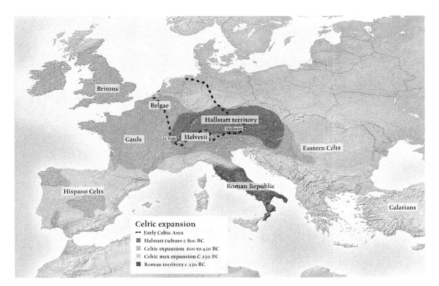

Celtic expansion
-- Early Celtic Area
☐ Hallstatt culture c 800 BC
☐ Celtic expansion 600 to 450 BC
☐ Celtic max expansion C 250 BC
■ Roman territory c 250 BC

As you can see from the map above, the Celtic culture, whose lineal descendants populate today's Ireland, Scotland, and the French province of Brittany, spread across much of Europe, beginning in the area around today's small and beautiful Austrian town of Hallstatt and its salt mines, which made it rich in the age before coinage. As you can see, the Gauls were just one part of a larger culture, located roughly in the borders of today's modern France.

The Celts were not an empire. There were great commonalities, such as language, religion, and clothing, but the Celtic people were tribal. Occasionally, tribes would make alliances for defensive or aggressive purposes and for economic reasons. Sometimes, a popular or powerful local leader would unite a group of tribes for a time. But overall, the Celtic tribes existed autonomously.

The map above shows you not only the expansion of Celtic culture but also the area of Italy that was controlled by the Roman Republic circa 250 BCE. Over the next 200 years, the Romans would expand into other areas of the Mediterranean, the North African coast, and the Middle East, enveloping the cultures of those areas into the Roman Empire (which, it must be remembered, was not led by an emperor until the ascension of Julius Caesar's nephew Octavian, known more widely as Augustus).

Julius Caesar's dreams of becoming the first Roman emperor became less of a dream and more of a reality in one place—Gaul.

Chapter 3 – Vercingetorix

When Julius Caesar was named the governor of the Roman province of Gaul in 58 BCE, Roman rule in the area hardly amounted to much. Though they claimed much of today's France, the Romans really only controlled the Mediterranean coast and the area along the Rhine River, and that was tenuous at the best of times in 58 BCE.

In many ways, the Romans were an advanced culture compared to the Gauls. They were unified where the Gallic tribes were divided. The Romans' skill at organizing men was unsurpassed in Europe (and perhaps the world) at the time. The Romans excelled at architecture, road-building, and much else. They had a trade network that brought them riches from one end of the known world to the other. Their armies were second to none in Europe and the Middle East.

Generally speaking, when the Romans approached a new people, they gave them a few choices. One was to submit to Roman rule and accept their government and taxation/tribute system. In return, these people had access to the greatest trading network in the world, as well as Roman protection. The other choice was to fight. This was often tantamount to genocide, as happened to Carthage in the Third Punic War in 146 BCE.

The Romans described the Gauls as "barbarians," which was exactly how the Greeks had described the Romans centuries before. The Latin word for "barbarian" is *barbara*, which stems from the Greek *barbaros*. Like the Greeks before them, the Romans used that word to mean anyone who was not a Roman citizen. The Greek and Latin meanings of the word are "foreign," "non-Greek/Roman," or "strange." Yes, it likely was used as a pejorative by Romans and Greeks at times, but the true essence of the word did not mean what we think of as "barbarian" today, though writers, painters, and filmmakers (until recently) have portrayed the tribes of Gaul and other non-Roman parts of Europe as primitive savages living in dark forests, perhaps one step up from cavemen.

That impression of the Gauls (and the tribes of Germany and Great Britain) came from the Romans, whose writings on the subject were extensive and almost the sole source of contemporary information we have on the people of present-day France, Belgium, Holland, Britain, and Germany.

Of course, since Rome was, well, Rome, and there were no competing sources of information (the tribes had very rudimentary alphabets, if any at all), we have a biased vision of what the Gallic tribes were like. For centuries, historians have put together a picture of Gaul based on Roman writings, with the foremost among them being Julius Caesar's recollections of his war in Gaul.

As pointed out above, the Romans had the most advanced civilization in Europe at the time. There was much about Rome that the Gallic tribes could barely comprehend. The size of the Roman Empire alone would have been mystifying for many of the Gauls and other tribes. The architecture and art would have been absolutely stunning, not just in the sense of beauty but stunning enough to be almost magical. Nothing like the statuary and art of Rome existed in Gaul. Nor did the roads, political administration, etc.

Historians of the time were hardly unbiased. From the time of the first great Roman historians, such as Sallust (86 BCE–35 BCE) and Livy (59 BCE-17 CE), Roman historians propped up the Roman Republic or Roman Empire, castigating its enemies and those Romans seen as being on the wrong side of whatever opinion the writer held. One of the more notable things about Roman histories is that they frequently express admiration for enemies or enemy leaders that (at least in Roman eyes) fought and likely died with bravery.

The Roman view of the Gauls was the prevalent view that is still held even today. That view essentially sees the Gauls as living in their tribal areas, almost as nomadic woodsmen. Typically, one thinks of the Gauls as living in the dark forests and hills, following game and living in primitive huts, tents, or even caves.

Most likely, Roman writers (including Caesar) knew this was not the correct picture, but this image of the Gauls served an important purpose. Portraying the Gauls and others as savages gave the Romans "permission" to conquer the "barbarians." After all, the "uncivilized" tribes presented a threat to Rome, or at least this was what the Romans said.

Illustration 7: Brennus and His Share of the Spoils, *painting by Paul Jamin, 1893.* Images like this not only titillated Victorian sensibilities but also spread the image of barbarian Gauls and civilized Romans.

Roman writers, politicians, generals, and the governing upper classes also told themselves that any invasion of Gaul was, in a way, "for the Gauls' own good." In their mind, they were bringing the Gauls "civilization," and they knew that the Gauls would eventually see the error of their ways, much like rebellious children eventually grow into cooperative adults.

We know from recent archaeological discoveries in France and throughout Celtic Europe that the Gauls and the other Celtic tribes of central and western Europe were much more sophisticated than was believed. Rather than being the semi-nomadic forest-dwelling people that the Romans believed (or wanted their public to believe) they were, the Gauls had an extensive trade network that reached from the Atlantic to the Danube. These trade routes consisted of roads (albeit dirt or laid stone, not the paved roads of the Romans) and river systems.

One of the ways we know this is the minted coins the Gauls left behind, as well as images on some pottery. Many times, these images were of horses, which played an obviously large part in Gallic life at the time, not only for travel and transport but also within Celtic mythology. In differing areas of Celtic Europe, horses were portrayed differently. Archaeologists have found Celtic coins with these localized styles in other parts of Europe, indicating both an advanced and extensive trade network. We know from Roman sources and other finds that the Celts traded in salt, grain, skins, meat, timber, wooden goods (wagons, etc.), cloth, and more.

Illustration 8: Celtic horses.

To some Gauls, the Roman way of life had its appeal. By forming alliances with Rome, they had better access to Roman trade routes, knowledge, and military power. Having the Romans as allies meant that certain tribal chiefs could exert inordinate power over their enemies and/or competitors, which, of course, was part of the Roman plan.

Unfortunately for both the Romans and the Gauls, Rome was hard to satisfy. In return for Roman protection and access to more Roman trade, the Gauls were required to pay ever-increasing amounts of tribute to Rome. In return, the Gauls seemed to receive ever-lessening benefits and ever-increasing demands for more. These demands also included demands for slaves, which the Gauls took from each other and presented to the Romans. At times, the Romans required Gallic chieftains to give up their sons for "education" in Rome, which was a way to subvert the Gallic culture.

Of course, much of this was intentional, as the Romans were the masters of the phrase "divide and conquer." Gaul promised untold riches, resources, and men. If they could make Gaul part of the Roman Republic (soon to be Roman Empire), then most of Europe would be theirs, and their position as the world's preeminent power might be assured. Gaul would also act as a stepping stone to other parts of the world, mainly Britain and Germany.

However, the Gauls, like others before them and others afterward, eventually had enough. That's where Vercingetorix (82 BCE–46 BCE) stepped into history.

Vercingetorix was the son of the Arverni tribe's tribe, and he lived in the area of today's southern France, specifically in the Auvergne region around the modern city of Clermont-Ferrand and the Massif Central mountainous region. Vercingetorix's father, Celtillus, had been elected the nominal chieftain of the Gauls in the region, but he was later put to death for trying to establish a Gallic kingdom with himself at its head. The Gauls were known to be fiercely independent, with each tribe existing independently except in times of great danger.

In 58 BCE, Julius Caesar was named the governor of the Roman province of Gallia Narbonensis, today's famous Provence region. The region had been taken by the Romans in 121 BCE after the Gauls staged an uprising against increasing Roman settlement in the area. Over the course of the next few years, Caesar, who was a master not only of military matters but also political ones, instituted a policy of "divide and conquer" in Gaul, which he combined with the "carrot and stick" approach. Some of the Gauls, hypnotized both by Roman power and riches, received positions of power from Caesar and lorded it over their cousins in other tribes. But the weaker the Gauls became, the stronger the Romans became. Roman settlement and military power in the area increased and expanded away from the coastal areas.

Over the course of Caesar's time in Gaul, many other Gauls were beginning to understand the Romans' intentions—that with the success of Roman ways came the end of the Gallic way of life.

In 52 BCE, a Gallic tribe called the Carnutes, whose territory in central France was beginning to be invaded by Roman settlements, rose up against the foreigners and slaughtered as many of them as they could. Vercingetorix and many of his followers and dependents (he was a prince, after all) were eager to join the revolt. He believed the Romans would only get more powerful over time and that the time was ripe, for events in Rome (chiefly the power struggles between Caesar's followers and Pompey's followers) had Caesar and the Romans in Gaul focused on events at home.

Unfortunately for Vercingetorix, a large number of other Gallic leaders, including his own uncle, believed that the Romans were simply too powerful to be challenged. Vercingetorix was sent into a kind of exile with his followers, but he returned to his tribe's capital city (then called Gergovia, today's Clermont-Ferrand) with an army of poor peasants and younger tribal leaders and took over the city.

By all accounts, Vercingetorix was a charismatic and skillful leader. Like many leaders then and now, he could also be harsh and brutal. He sent out messengers and met with other Gallic tribal leaders from throughout the region and other parts of Gaul, cajoling, convincing, and threatening them to unite against the Romans.

Caesar had spies and well-paid allies among the Gauls, so he was kept apprised of Vercingetorix's plans to unite the tribes. Small battles between Romans and Gauls led by Vercingetorix had resulted in Roman victories, and Caesar was determined to crush the rebellion by seizing a major city and granary, what the Romans called an *oppidum* (a settlement), called Avaricum (present-day Bourges).

Vercingetorix knew that Caesar was headed toward Avaricum, and he proceeded to burn every single grain he could find for fifteen miles around the town. The residents of Avaricum begged Vercingetorix not to burn their city to the ground, and realizing that the town and area around it was defensible, the Gallic leader left it intact.

Over the next month, the Romans besieged Avaricum. While they were doing so, Vercingetorix's cavalry and other units harassed them endlessly. Combined with their slowly dwindling food supply and growing hunger, the Romans, when they finally breached the city walls, killed virtually every person in Avaricum. According to Caesar's writings, they killed an estimated 40,000 people and left only about 800 alive.

If the Romans believed the slaughter at Avaricum would cow the Gauls, they were wrong. If they wanted to anger the Gallic rebels and draw them into battle, they got their wish. Caesar had about ten legions with him in southern Gaul (around 40,000 to 60,000 soldiers). To prevent the tribes of northern Gaul from joining Vercingetorix, he sent six legions northward to block any northerners from moving south. With his remaining forces, Caesar moved toward Gergovia, the capital of Vercingetorix's tribe, the Arverni. This took place in the late winter of 52 BCE

After a series of maneuvers and counter-moves, Caesar's forces attempted to take control of the town's water supply. When they did, his allies, the Aedui, turned on him, as agreed with Vercingetorix, and a costly battle began. Caesar defeated the Aedui and moved toward the town with the remainder of his forces. As he did, Vercingetorix led a massive cavalry charge into Roman lines, then dismounted and joined the remaining Aedui in attacking the Romans on foot. Caesar recorded his losses at several hundred officers and men, but modern historians think it was much more, closer to perhaps several thousand. Caesar, who was nearly surrounded on the hilltop where Gergovia lay, ordered a retreat.

Gergovia was an important victory for the Gauls, as it resulted in many other tribes joining forces with Vercingetorix. Over the course of the next few months, Vercingetorix and the rulers of the other tribes trained the armies of Gaul for the fight they knew was coming. Vercingetorix was reputedly a harsh leader. He trained his men relentlessly in more modern tactics and punished laziness and insubordination severely, for he knew that defeat at the hands of the Romans likely meant slavery or death for many of his people. At the same time, Caesar summoned 10,000 men from the Teutonic (German) tribes along the Rhine River and recalled his other Roman legions southward.

By September, Vercingetorix's forces numbered about 80,000 men. They had fought a number of smaller battles with the Romans and had been defeated in virtually all of them. The Gauls fell back to the fortified town of Alesia and awaited the Romans' next moves. Caesar, inflating the Gallic forces for his own political purposes, numbered them at 250,000. The Roman forces themselves numbered an estimated 60,000.

Alesia was set on a hillside with rivers on both sides. Around the town, the Gauls had dug trenches and erected a large stone wall. Recognizing its strength, Caesar knew that a frontal attack was doomed to fail and ordered his troops to begin a siege. They dug an amazing eleven miles of trenches around the Alesia *oppidum*, which were connected by twenty-three strong points.

Vercingetorix knew there was only about thirty days' worth of supplies in the town, so he sent his cavalry out through a gap in the Roman lines one moonless night, hoping they would reach the forces of other Gauls in the area to aid the town. Caesar learned of these plans from prisoners his men had taken and set about preparing an additional set of trench and fortifications three miles outside of his lines, facing the town.

Sometime later, Vercingetorix's hopes were achieved when a large relief force of Gauls was sighted in the distance, but on the first day of battle, which lasted from dawn to dusk, the Roman forces and their German allies were able to prevent the Gallic reinforcements from breaking through their lines to relieve Alesia.

On the second day of the battle, the Gauls inside Alesia and those outside assaulted the two Roman lines. While Vercingetorix's forces made a little progress, they received word that their allies had been repulsed again on the Roman lines miles from the town.

The third day of the battle was the key. Both Vercingetorix and Caesar personally took part in combat, leading their men at dangerous moments. The Gauls outside the city broke through a gap in the Roman lines and were threatening to join with Vercingetorix, but in a series of quick-thinking and rapid moves, Caesar succeeded in surrounding this large force of Gauls and almost completely wiped it out. Those men who survived ran in panic to the remainder of their forces outside the town and caused them to flee. That left just Vercingetorix and his dwindling number of men in the town.

That night, Vercingetorix called together all of the Gallic leaders in Alesia and asked them how they wanted to proceed. Did they want to kill him, or did they want him to surrender to Caesar? Hoping to appease Caesar with the surrender of their leader, the Gauls told Vercingetorix to give himself up the next day, which he did.

Illustration 9: Vercingetorix surrendering to Caesar. A painting by Lionel Royer, who based the scene on Caesar's description.

Because Caesar respected Vercingetorix and because the Arverni had fought with great bravery, Caesar spared most of the tribe from slavery or death, but many of the other Gallic tribes were not so fortunate. As a lesson to the Gauls and as a concession to his men (whose support he would need for his future plans), Caesar gave many of the survivors to his troops as slaves. Over the next four and a half years, Caesar and the Romans would settle more of their countrymen in Gaul, and most of Gaul would become part of the Roman Republic. Alesia allowed Julius Caesar to become the legend he is today.

As for Vercingetorix, he spent those next five and a half years as a Roman prisoner. In Caesar's triumphal marches on his return home, Vercingetorix was displayed before roaring crowds in Rome, then taken back to prison and strangled, per the Roman custom.

Vercingetorix's image was rehabilitated during the time of Napoleon and his nephew, Napoleon III. His image as a fierce French/Gallic warrior was just what the two 19th-century French emperors needed. Napoleon III had a massive statue of Vercingetorix erected near the town of Clermont-Ferrand, near Vercingetorix's capital, where it still stands today.

Chapter 4 – Charlemagne

Some 852 years later, a new Roman emperor would be crowned in Rome. The circumstances of this coronation were vastly different than that which existed at the dawning of the Roman Empire with the naming of Julius Caesar's nephew, Octavian, as the first Roman emperor, Augustus Caesar, but the ritual sent the same message: "I am the most powerful man in Europe."

The man being made emperor was not Roman, and there wasn't truly a "Roman Empire" to rule over, but in 800 CE, the pope and the emperor-to-be decided that the title was fitting and that it was likely needed to bring back some semblance of order to a western Europe that had fallen into darkness since the end of the real Roman Empire centuries before.

That new emperor was Charlemagne or, in Latin, *Karolus*, and he was a Frank, meaning he was neither a Roman nor a Gaul. The Franks were a Germanic tribe that had settled on both sides of the Rhine River sometime in the 3rd century CE, and both France and Germany have claimed Charlemagne's legacy for their own in more recent times.

In the centuries between the Roman conquest of Gaul and the rise of Charlemagne, the population of what is now France, as well as parts of Belgium, Luxembourg, Switzerland, and western Germany, changed almost completely. The Roman conquest of Gaul was so complete that a new culture, "Gallo-Roman," was born. Of course, this meant not only the spread of Roman culture and its incorporation into Gaul but also the spread of Roman DNA and vice versa. Though millennia have passed, even today, traces of Roman influence can be seen in the French population, especially on the southern coast, where, very generally speaking, the people have darker hair and more olive skin than their northern brothers and sisters.

The Gauls who remained outside of the Roman sphere of influence were located as far as possible from the Romans as they could be while still being in Gaul/France. These were, and are, the people of Brittany, which is the French province that borders the English Channel in the northwest and the Atlantic to the south and east. Even the name "Brittany" is Celtic, and it is linguistically related to the words "Britain" and "Britons" (the name for the many tribes of England and Wales that lived there before the Romans arrived in that country). Though the Bretons (the modern French word for the distinct people of Brittany) are French citizens, many still speak a unique language, and you will see road signs throughout the region in both French, Breton, and occasionally Gallo. The last two languages are members of the Celtic language tree that includes Gaelic, the native language of Ireland.

The Germanic tribes known collectively as the Franks made their home in the Lower Rhine area. "Lower" in this case is actually north, not south, as the rivers in western Europe, with the exception of the Danube, which really begins in central Europe, flow from south to north. The Lower Rhine is in the area of today's Belgium, part of Holland, and the part of France known as Flanders.

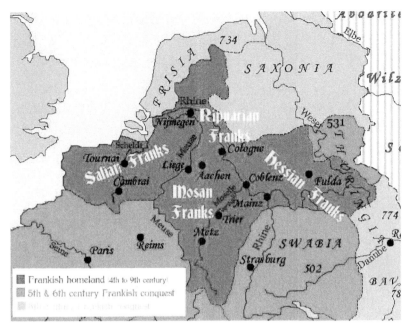

Illustration 10: The Frankish homeland in dark green. Map courtesy of Eupedia.com, an excellent site for those interested in deep research into European genetic genealogy.

For our purposes, the more significant of the four groups above are the Salian Franks (a word that describes their location near the North Sea) and the Ripuarian Franks (*ripuarian* connoting "river," in this case, the Rhine). The location of the Franks' homeland was unfortunate in some ways.

We know that the Romans had contact with them before the 3ʳᵈ century CE, which was when the name "Frank" began to be used in Roman writings. The Romans had conducted trade with the Franks, and a significant number of Franks were in the Roman army, especially in the later years of the empire.

On their northern borders, both the Salian and Ripuarian Franks were faced with the Saxons, which was a rival and quite warlike Germanic tribe. By the 3ʳᵈ century, Rome's power was in decline, and those living in the Roman settlements along the Rhine River were frequently the subject of powerful raids from the Saxons and their allies to the east. As a result, the Romans, along with their Frankish allies, relocated farther west, away from the Saxon homeland and into more defensible and populated areas.

As the power of the Romans became even weaker in the 5th century, the Franks began to assert themselves on the left bank of the Rhine River. In 462, the Ripuarian Franks took Cologne, one of the largest Roman cities in Gaul/France.

In the middle of the 5th century, one Frankish family became dominant. This was the Merovingian family, who took their name from a legendary Salian Frankish king named Merovech, who purportedly took part in the Battle of Chalons, also known as the Battle of the Catalaunian Plains, in 451. In this battle, an allied army of Romans, Goths, and Franks defeated the forces of Attila the Hun, preventing them from driving into France.

The grandson of Merovech, Clovis I, was the founder of a united Frankish kingdom after killing most of his powerful rivals. By the 480s/490s, Clovis had conquered most of Gaul with the exception of the powerful Burgundians and the Ripuarian Franks. By 509, he was proclaimed the king of all the Franks when he seized Cologne from the Ripuarians, He died in 511, and he set a poor precedent by dividing his kingdom between his four sons, likely in the hope that they would work together. This was not to be.

After a century of divided rule, the Merovingians united behind Clotaire II to form a single Frankish kingdom. In those one hundred years and after the death of Clotaire's son Dagobert I (r. 629–639), the Merovingian kings, for many reasons (including weak personalities, infighting, and giving more attention to luxury than ruling), saw their power decline in favor of their chancellors, known to history as the mayors of the palace.

Of these mayors of the palace, the most significant were Pepin II, also known as Pepin the Middle or Pepin of Herstal (b. 635–d. 714), and his grandson, Pepin the Short (b. 714–d. 768).

Pepin II came to rule the Franks in all but name after defeating the forces of the other powerful mayors in the divided Merovingian kingdom. He ruled from 687 to his death in 714, and he ceded power to his son, Charles Martel, known to history as Charles the Hammer (*Martel* means "hammer" in the Frankish language). A more apt name would be hard to find in history.

Illustration 11: Charles Martel at Tours.

The early Merovingian kings, as well as their mayors of the palace, were known for their ruthlessness. Charles the Hammer might have been the most ruthless of them all. Of course, he needed to be, for throughout his young life, people, including his stepmother, were trying to kill him.

The story of Charles is long, but for our purposes here, he is important for two reasons. The first is his defeat of the Moors at Tours. The Muslim Arab armies, which had stormed out of the Arabian Peninsula after the revelations of the Prophet Muhammad, were referred to as the Moors by contemporary historians. By defeating the Moors at Tours, Martel prevented the spread of Islam into the rest of Europe (the Moors had conquered Spain in 711). Charles also subdued the tribes of Saxony and extended the Frankish Empire into the southern part of modern-day Germany, placing puppet kings in each area. Both of these territories would give Charles's grandson trouble. The second major reason Charles Martel is remembered is that he was the founder of the Carolingian dynasty. His son, Pepin the Short, became the first Carolingian king, and his grandson, the great Charlemagne, followed in his father's footsteps.

By the time of Charlemagne's birth, the Franks had established themselves as the most powerful European dynasty outside of the Byzantine Empire, but it was Charlemagne that would make the Franks a rival to anyone on the Continent. He was born on April 2nd, but his birth year is unclear. Some have it as 742, others 747, and still others 748. He died at the considerable age of sixty-five (if one goes with 742 as his birth year). Back then, the average lifespan was between thirty and thirty-five.

We know very little about Charlemagne's early life, though a great deal can be at least somewhat accurately surmised. Being a prince, he was well educated for his time. He spoke his native language, and he could also speak Latin and understand Greek. He was given as much education about the world outside of Frankish domains as was known. For his entire life, Charlemagne pursued knowledge, bringing in experts on many subjects to study and write at his court. The years between the fall of the Roman Empire (c. 400) and the start of the Renaissance (c. 1300) are often referred to as the Dark Ages, for it was believed that in those centuries, the progress made by the Greeks and Romans had been lost and forgotten. Until the latter part of the 20th century, historians had a tendency to portray this time as a bleak, barbaric, and ignorant time, and in a lot of ways, it was. However, while much of the knowledge of the Greeks and Romans was lost to most of Europe, much of it was kept in the former Roman provinces in the Middle East and Egypt, as well as in the court of the Byzantine Empire. The "rediscovery" of this knowledge by Europeans in the 12th century and its application and expansion led to the Renaissance. But in the vaults of the Catholic Church in Rome and in churches and monasteries throughout Europe, much of that knowledge remained, and the kings and queens of Europe, like Charlemagne, had access to it if they wanted it badly enough. Charlemagne certainly did. By all accounts, his appetite for knowledge was unbounded.

Charlemagne's hunger for knowledge was not limited to the study of languages and the sciences (such as they were at the time), as he also craved to learn of his kingdom. As both king and emperor, Charlemagne spent much of his life traveling to the far reaches of his lands. He did this sometimes out of military necessity, but he often traveled to the courts of his underlings to make sure that things were happening as he was told, to make sure his deputies knew he was watching them, and to find out both the problems and assets of his lands firsthand. Additionally, it has recently been brought to light that Charlemagne had a vast, well-organized, and powerful network of spies and informants throughout both his lands and, in some cases, the lands of his enemies.

Charlemagne was able to keep this network strong in a few ways. Firstly, he was the wealthiest ruler in Europe (excluding the Byzantines, much of whose empire at the time was outside the Continent). He paid handsomely for both information and loyalty. Secondly, he had spies watching his spies, which is a quite modern idea. Thirdly, Charlemagne inspired loyalty, as he was a charismatic and intelligent figure. Fourth, in addition to being charismatic and intelligent, he was also ruthless. In this case, the name "Dark Ages" is apropos. Torture was not the exception in the 8th and 9th centuries—it was the rule.

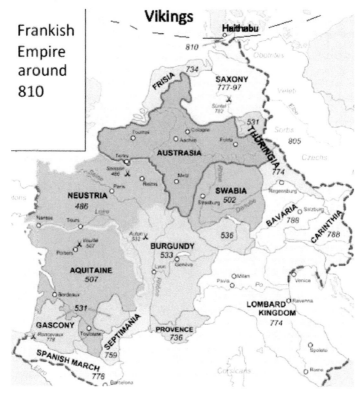

Illustration 12: The evolution of the Frankish Empire with dates of expansion.

When Pepin the Short died in September 768, his domain was given not to his eldest son Charlemagne but to both Charlemagne and his other son, Carloman. They were to rule as co-equals, though each was to govern specific regions. Generally speaking, Charlemagne governed the outer parts of the kingdom bordering the seas, except in the south. Carloman governed the interior part of modern-day France down to the Mediterranean and bordering on today's northern Italy.

This arrangement must have rankled Charlemagne to a degree, and he spent much of his early reign outwardly accepting the situation but maneuvering behind the scenes to box his brother in both politically and geographically, moving in his own allies to areas ostensibly under his younger brother's control. Not only was Carloman nine years younger than Charlemagne, but he was also hardly experienced in all the ways that mattered at the time. Mostly, this meant at war. By the time the brothers came to rule Francia, Charlemagne had been fighting battles throughout the kingdom at his father's side or behest.

For many years, historians suspected that Charlemagne had his brother murdered. We do know that Carloman died shortly after a major disagreement between the two brothers, but it seems that this was a coincidence. Although we don't know for certain what killed Carloman, it was more likely he died from complications from a peptic ulcer than at his brother's hand.

The brothers' disagreement arose over what to do about unrest in the southwest of France, in one of the richest and most fertile areas of the country known as Aquitaine. It was named after an ancient tribe, the Aquitani, who were likely related to today's Basques. It is thought the Basque language and the language spoken by the people in the area, also known as Aquitani, were related. Aquitani is a dead language today.

From 759 to 768, the people of Aquitaine fought a brutal war against Charlemagne and Carloman's father, Pepin the Short. A year later, the Aquitanians invaded Frankish territory, seeking both revenge and attempting to divide Charlemagne and Carloman. The brothers argued over what to do. Charlemagne was in favor of putting down the Aquitanians, which Carloman opposed. Charlemagne led a successful campaign against the Aquitanians, and through a series of negotiations, he allowed their leader, Hunald II, to live out the rest of his life peacefully in a monastery. All of Hunald's men swore allegiance to the Franks, more specifically to Charlemagne. As a result, the territory was finally and irrevocably made part of the Frankish Empire.

Throughout his time as the joint king of the Franks, Charlemagne was advised by his wise and impressive mother, Bertrada of Laon (a city about eighty-five miles northeast of Paris). Bertrada clearly favored Charlemagne over his younger brother and counseled the former in his attempts to nullify Carloman's influence. Bertrada also greatly influenced Charlemagne's love life. Perhaps "love life" is the wrong term. Bertrada instructed Charlemagne on forming political alliances through marriage.

Charlemagne's first wife, Himiltrude, gave him one son, Pepin the Hunchback, who would later lead an abortive revolt against his father. After the birth of Pepin, Bertrada counseled Charlemagne to marry Desiderata, the daughter of the powerful king of the Lombards, Desiderius, in order to gain a powerful ally and further surround Carloman's territories. Apparently, however, Desiderata was not Charlemagne's cup of tea, for he soon divorced her to marry Hildegard, a Frankish princess.

Desiderius was furious at this slight and vowed to make life miserable for Charlemagne. Step one would have been to ally himself with Carloman, but it was at this moment that Carloman passed away, allowing Charlemagne to become the sole ruler of the Franks. And as soon as he had become king in his own right, he was involved in international power politics.

In 772, Adrian I was named the new pope. One of the new pope's first acts was to demand the return of former papal territories near the city of Ravenna and some farther south. These former papal territories had first been seized by armies of the Byzantine Empire and then lost to the Lombards when they moved into northern Italy from their homeland in what is now northern Germany. The Lombards had reached an agreement with the papacy that they would return these territories upon Desiderius's ascension to the throne, but when he became king, Desiderius instead marched toward Rome, intent on taking much of Italy, including Rome, for himself.

Charlemagne's father, Pepin, had supported the papacy in the negotiations with the Lombards, so Adrian I appealed to Charlemagne to do the same. The Frankish king was a devout Catholic, despite his many wives and concubines, and sent ambassadors to support the pope in negotiations with the Lombards. In the end, Charlemagne demanded the return of the territories, and Desiderius, as you can imagine, adamantly refused.

Charlemagne then conducted a brilliant campaign and besieged the Lombard capital city of Pavia for much of 774. In the end, Charlemagne defeated not only Desiderius but also his son, Adelchis, who attempted to relieve the city. Desiderius was forced into a monastery, and his son escaped to live in exile in Byzantium. This left Charlemagne in control of northern Italy, which was the strongest power in the country. He crowned himself the king of Lombardy and gave control of the disputed cities to the pope. Two years later, he interrupted another campaign in Germany to return to Italy to put down a rebellion, and with that, Charlemagne was the undisputed master of the Italian Peninsula, France, and much of southwestern Germany.

Illustration 13: Growth of the Frankish Empire. Charlemagne's additions are in light grey-green.

As you can see from the map above, Charlemagne was at war with the Germanic tribes for decades. The most troublesome and prolonged struggles the king faced throughout his long reign were with the Saxons in northern Germany, and it is there that the deeds of Charlemagne have come under the most scrutiny in recent years.

In the whole of Saxony and in parts of northern Thuringia and the coastal territory of Frisia, the people worshiped the Germanic gods of Odin, Thor, Frey, and Freya, among others. As a devoted and zealous Catholic, Charlemagne was determined not only to add Saxony to his empire but also to stamp out the pagan religion in both territories once and for all.

Charlemagne's armies were large for the time. Contemporary writings and reports numbered his armies at 100,000, but modern historians put it closer to 30,000 or 40,000, which was still large for its time. Charlemagne warred against the Saxons in 772, 785, 792 to 793, and from 798 to 803. As you can see, the struggle against the Saxons was long, and it became extremely brutal. Throughout the campaigns, especially in the last one, Charlemagne and his men forcibly converted the Saxons to Christianity.

In the first years of his war against the Saxons, Charlemagne would be satisfied when Saxon leaders swore allegiance to him and renounced their pagan religion. In some instances, Saxon leaders would remain loyal to Charlemagne, who, in return for loyalty and conversion, could be generous. However, many Saxons who converted at the end of a spear soon turned their backs on Christianity when the Franks left. The Frankish army usually had to fight in other areas of the empire, for instance, against the Muslims on the Spanish border or in central Europe against the Avars, a nomadic tribe that had settled in what is now modern-day Austria, Hungary, and parts of Serbia.

In the later campaigns against the Saxons, Charlemagne was ruthless. In 782, his troops slaughtered over 4,000 Saxons who refused to convert. All throughout Saxony, people were forced to convert. The Franks used the Saxons' loyalty against them, forcing their children into learning a Christian education and encouraging them to report on their parents or anyone else who practiced pagan rituals or espoused pagan beliefs in private. Anyone accused or caught in the act of worshiping pagan gods or conducting pagan rituals was often put to death, sometimes in very slow and painful ways. The last Saxon rebellion against Christianity and Charlemagne's rule was in 804, over thirty years after the Frankish king had first made war against them.

Frankish expansion ended at the modern Danish border. In the latter years of Charlemagne's reign, Danish and Norwegian Vikings had begun small-scale raids of Frankish territory, but the Vikings were a more significant problem for Charlemagne's heirs than the emperor himself.

Holy Roman Emperor

On Christmas Day of the year 800, Pope Leo III crowned Charlemagne as the emperor of the Romans. The title of Holy Roman emperor would live on until 1918, by which time it had long lost any real meaning.

However, in 800, the title was fraught with meaning in a number of ways. Pope Leo was an unpopular pope, and he was almost killed by a Roman mob in 799 after being accused of adultery and perjury by relatives of the former pope, Adrian I. Leo's family was not a noble one, and this, too, made him many enemies, as they believed that only nobility should hold the highest position in the church. Because of Charlemagne's power and his devout Christianity, Leo fled to Charlemagne's court, which was then at Paderborn in today's Germany.

Charlemagne knew that any rift in the Roman Catholic Church was likely to have serious effects through his realm and elsewhere. A divided Catholic Europe would only become weaker, making it an even greater target for the Muslims in Spain and the Eastern Orthodox Christians of the Byzantine Empire. The Byzantine emperors had long laid claim to authority in Rome and considered themselves the heirs of the Roman Empire itself.

Charlemagne called a synod, which is a meeting of clergymen, in Rome, with himself presiding, to determine Leo's innocence or guilt. The long and short of it is that Leo swore an oath to Charlemagne that he was innocent, and Charlemagne accepted it. Since Charlemagne controlled most of Italy with his army, the attending clergy fell into line.

Now seen as dependent on Charlemagne, Pope Leo contrived to raise the office of pope back to its former stature. He then announced his intent to crown Charlemagne as *Imperator Romanum,* or "Emperor of the Romans." Since it was the pope doing the crowning, the intended impression was for Europe to see it as the pope who had the ultimate power, not Charlemagne.

Centuries later, during WWII, British Prime Minister Winston Churchill suggested to Soviet leader Josef Stalin that it might be a good idea to invite the pope to the Tehran Conference of 1943, where issues regarding the war and post-war Europe were to be made. Stalin's reply perfectly fits the situation between Pope Leo and Charlemagne in 800. Stalin replied, "The Pope? How many divisions does he have?"

In 800, as in 1943, everyone knew where the real power lay: Charlemagne. Still, it put the Frankish ruler in a strange position. Firstly, he was in negotiations with the Byzantines, mainly its empress, Irene, who was eligible for marriage. Charlemagne had grand plans for his empire, as he wanted to unite both the Western and Eastern Empires into a renewed Roman Empire with himself at its head. By accepting the crown from the pope, Charlemagne undermined his negotiations by not taking into consideration the position of the Byzantines. Some historians, therefore, believe that had Charlemagne known what the pope was going to do, he would not have entered the hall that day. However, others believe that Charlemagne was well aware of the pope's intentions and knew it would add an extra dimension to his power, as he would become the defender of Western Christendom.

With his ascension to Holy Roman emperor and with his armies in possession of most of western Europe and significant areas of central Europe, Charlemagne is considered by many to be the forefather of the idea of a "United Europe." Today, that idea is represented, for better or worse, by the European Union. But others with less benevolent intent have held Charlemagne up as a role model, including Hitler and a Frenchmen of the late 18th and early 19th centuries that we shall be telling you about later.

Illustration 14: Charlemagne as depicted by Albrecht Durer (1471-1528). In the upper left is the symbol of the Holy Roman Empire, and the upper right depicts the symbol of the kings of France.

Chapter 5 – A Collision of Cultures, 814–1429

As you may have noticed, we are using a number of famous individuals as the foundation for this brief history of France. French history is so rich, so influential, and so detailed that writing a 150-page book can swiftly turn into a 400-page book in the blink of an eye.

However, in order to understand the situation facing France and our next major protagonist, we are going to have to include a chapter covering the years between the death of Charlemagne and the situation facing France in the early 1400s.

Knowing he was dying, Charlemagne named his son Louis (known as Louis the Pious) as the king of the Franks and the co-emperor of the Holy Roman Empire. Louis had also been given charge of Aquitaine in 781, and in that position, he had reclaimed much of northern Spain from the Muslims. By the time of his father's death in early 814, he had considerable experience in both ruling and warfare.

Unfortunately for Louis, he had three sons, each of whom wanted to be king, and much of Louis's later reign was a time of civil war. In fact, there were three great uprisings involving his sons and their allies in their quest for power. Unfortunately for his sons, Louis was a skilled warrior. During the long civil wars, each son allied with his father or at least made peace with him only to wage war on the others.

When Louis the Pious died in 840, the brothers all warred upon each other again for three years, but none of them was able to get the upper hand. Of course, in all of this violence between royal brothers and their allies, the common people suffered.

In 843, the brothers met at the town of Verdun in today's eastern France. There, the brothers hammered out an agreement to divide the empire among them. The eldest of Louis's children, Lothair I, was given control over what is known as Middle Francia, and he was also given the title of Holy Roman emperor, as he had been so designated by their father. This title, however, did not give Lothair any control over his brothers or their lands. On the following page, you will see a map illustrating the division of the empire.

Louis the Pious's middle son, Louis II, is known to history as Louis the German, and you can probably guess why. He was given control of the eastern part of the empire, which encompassed modern-day Germany. In German, "Louis" is "Ludwig," as you will see on the map below.

Lastly, the youngest son, Charles the Bald, was given the largest and perhaps richest portion of the empire: western France, with the exception of Brittany, which was under the control of its own powerful dukes.

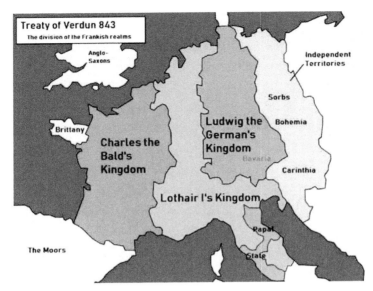

This division of the Carolingian Empire is regarded by historians as the founding of France and Germany as we have come to know them. Though many similarities remained, it was at this point that new cultural and political customs appeared, as well as two new languages, French and German, though in much different forms than they exist today.

For our purposes here, Charles the Bald is our focus. Firstly, was he bald? It is not likely. Contemporary paintings of him show a man with a full head of hair, and accounts of his person describe someone very hairy indeed. The name may have been a sarcastic reference, or it might refer to an earlier meaning of the root of the word "bald," meaning "without land." As the youngest child of Louis, Charles did indeed have much less land than his brothers, at least for a time.

You might be familiar with Charles the Bald from the TV series *Vikings*. Like much of that series, the writers played fast and loose with the timelines and many of the facts, but they did get some of Charles's story right. He did have a daughter named Gisela or Gisla, but he - did not marry her off to Rollo, who is Ragnar's brother in the series. The real Rollo didn't live until long after Ragnar

Lothbrok, and it's still debated whether Ragnar existed at all. In the series, Charles is asked to appeal to his brothers for aid, which he initially refuses to do, then reports that he had but with no results. Whether this was true or not, his brothers likely would not have come to his aid, as they were bitter rivals even after the Treaty of Verdun. Lastly, Charles the Bald fought the Vikings himself, relatively successfully. Charles's grandson was another Charles, this time called "the Simple." Initially, this nickname meant "straightforward"; one later writer called him Charles the Stupid for a battlefield error in 919. Charles the Simple was the man who actually gave Rollo land in western France, and it was Charles the Simple who had a daughter named Gisela or Gisla, whom he married to Rollo.

Rollo is where things get complicated. Rollo's history before he came to France is immaterial here. Let's just say he was a Viking—and a tall one at that. He was known as *Hrolf Gangr*, or "Rollo the Walker," for he is said to have been so tall that when seated on a horse, his legs touched the ground.

What we do know is that Rollo is a pivotal figure in history. He was a Viking chief, and by the time he besieged Paris and the city of Chartres in 911, he must have been a veteran warrior and highly regarded Viking chief. Though Rollo was defeated by Charles the Simple's army at Chartres, the French king decided to reach terms with Rollo to avoid further raids on his territories.

Rollo was given what became known as Normandy, which simply means "Land of the Northmen." In return, he swore loyalty to Charles, meaning he would fight for Charles when requested. This included fighting other Vikings, but Vikings fought against each other all the time. One of Rollo's first wars as the ruler of Normandy was against another Viking group that sought to take Normandy from him. Additionally, Rollo agreed to be baptized and bring his children up as Christians.

Rollo's great-great-great-grandson was William the Conqueror, although he didn't gain this epithet until later in life. By 1028, around the time William was born, Rollo's descendants had made Normandy the most powerful entity in France. Normandy was essentially a country unto itself. Rollo's descendants (shown below) developed a powerful army that was renowned throughout Europe for its prowess.

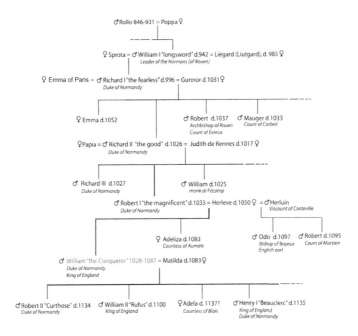

William, also known as "the Bastard" for his illegitimate birth, would become the duke of Normandy in 1035. In addition to that, he had a claim to the English throne as well. His first cousin once-removed was Edward the Confessor, the English king. A first cousin once-removed may seem a bit distant to be the heir to the English throne, but Edward was childless.

Also in the running to become the English king was Harold Godwinson, whose powerful noble family had been both rival and ally to Edward the Confessor. Harold became Edward's right-hand man later in the king's life and helped him put down numerous rebellions, including one by Harold's own brother. Edward fell into a coma in late 1065, but before he died, he regained consciousness and expressed his wish that Harold "protect" both his kingdom and his soon-to-be-widow. Harold took this as Edward's wish for him to be the next king, so he proceeded to gather the Witan (the Anglo-Saxon king's council), which voted to name him king, and he was crowned on January 6th, 1066.

Harold was immediately beset by problems, namely keeping his throne. Not only did the powerful William of Normandy claim the kingship of England but so did another formidable enemy, the man historians call the "last great Viking king," Harald Hardrada ("Hard-ruler") of Norway.

Harald's adventurous life could fill a book itself. It was he, not Ragnar Lothbrok, who staged his own death in order to help breach a besieged city's walls, and he had fought from Byzantium all across Europe. Now a king in Norway, Harald's claim was tenuous at best. He claimed descent from Cnut the Great, the Scandinavian Viking king who had become king not only of Denmark and Norway but also England and who had ruled from 1016 to 1035. Harald also claimed that Harold Godwinson's brother, Tostig, who had rebelled against his brother and King Edward and fled to Norway, promised him the kingship of England.

Muddying the waters even further, William of Normandy claimed that he had received Harold Godwinson's oath that Harold would support William's claim to the throne. This had allegedly (and probably) happened when Harold had gone across the English Channel in 1064. There are numerous theories as to why Harold went to France, but they are too numerous to discuss here. Suffice it to say that Harold was taken prisoner by the count of Ponthieu, an area south of Normandy, with the count likely hoping for a rich ransom from the Godwin family in England and perhaps the king himself. That was not to be, as William of Normandy personally went to Ponthieu and ordered Harold to be released. And William was not a man to be trifled with.

For the next few weeks, Harold made the acquaintance of William and even accompanied him in battle. He apparently rescued two of William's men from quicksand and generally acquitted himself well, whether it was in battle, drinking, or feasting. However, it was clear that Harold, despite the pleasurable surroundings, was William's prisoner, and what William seemed to want was a promise of Harold's support when it came time for William to claim the throne of England.

For those of you interested in this topic, there are many fascinating books on the subject, as well as the amazing Bayeux Tapestry, which was woven shortly after William's conquest of England and still survives today. Andrew Bridgeford's 1066: THE HIDDEN HISTORY IN THE BAYEUX TAPESTRY (2009) TELLS THE AMAZING TALE OF THE TAPESTRY, THE STORY OF WILLIAM AND HAROLD, AND MANY OTHER SECRETS WOVEN WITHIN THE CLOTH.

AS YOU CAN IMAGINE, WHEN HAROLD RETURNED TO ENGLAND, HE SOON FORGOT, OR AT LEAST DISMISSED, HIS OATH TO WILLIAM, WHICH WAS TAKEN UNDER DURESS. WILLIAM, ON THE OTHER HAND, DID NOT FORGET.

Illustration 15: Bayeux Tapestry: Harold gives his oath to William with his hand on two altars.

Upon hearing of harold's ascent to the kingship, william began preparations to invade england.

Harold godwinson was between a rock and a hard place, and in september 1066, his kingdom was invaded, but it was not by william. The first to strike was harald hardrada, who sailed with a large viking army and landed in the north of england near york. King harold of england moved northward with his army to meet the vikings, despite the many warnings that william and the normans (the far larger threat) were amassing a fleet on the norman coast. Harold was convinced he could march north, defeat the vikings, and then attend to william, if he even came.

Harold and harald hardrada met at stamford bridge just outside of york. The english defeated the vikings handily, and harald hardrada was killed in the battle. Many consider this the end of the viking age.

Unfortunately for harold of england, word came to him at stamford bridge that william had landed on the southern coast of england. He was counseled by some of his aides to rest his army before moving south, but harold was determined to meet william in battle before the normans could move too far inland.

As you may know, the two armies met at hastings in southern england on october 14th, 1066. Though the outcome hung in the balance for some time, william was eventually victorious, harold took an arrow to the eye and died, and the last successful invasion of england was a reality.

For the next nearly 400 years, the english, whose anglo-saxon culture was married (some would say forcibly) to norman french culture, controlled not only england but a significant portion of france as well, at times controlling almost half of that country either directly or through marriage and alliances, especially with the ruling families of burgundy. At times, the english kings attempted to assert tenuous claims to the french throne and even included the french royal coat of arms on their standards.

Illustration 16: The coat of arms of English king Henry V with Norman lions and French fleur-de-lys.

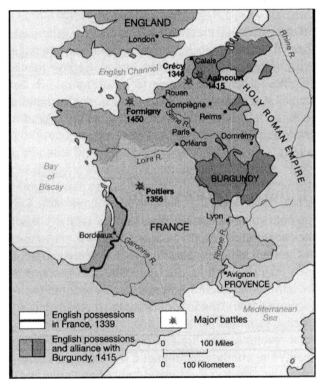

Illustration 17: English possessions in France during the Hundred Years' War. Joan of Arc made her appearance toward the end of this conflict.

Chapter 6 – Jeanne d'Arc

In August 1346, the English under Edward III, whose grandfather was the famous Edward I Longshanks of *Braveheart* (1995) fame and whose mother, Isabella, was the daughter of King Philip IV of France, defeated the armies of the French king at the famous Battle of Crécy. Crécy was a crushing defeat for the French, and it gave the English a much larger foothold in France, including the important and rich port of Calais.

Before we go any further, remember, *Braveheart* was a drama, and like the aforementioned TV series *Vikings*, and it was based in fact. In *Braveheart*, Edward I arranges a marriage to Isabella of France, but as you can see, she was married to his grandson, and when she came to England, she was only twelve. She also did not grow up into the kind, intelligent woman portrayed in the film but rather as the woman who became known as the She-Wolf of France and who ruled England along with her lover, Roger Mortimer, until Edward III put them in their places. For Isabella, it was a monastery. For Mortimer, it was the noose.

As you can see, the French and English, as well as the Burgundian ruling families, were all connected, which resulted in much confusion for later historians and a war that lasted one hundred years (give or take).

In 1356, the English won another great victory at Poitiers in Aquitaine. At both Crécy and Poitiers, the battle was decided by the English archers with their longbows, as they were deployed in large numbers. These bows, made from the wood of the yew tree, had an effective range of over 300 yards and could punch through almost any armor of the day given the right arrowhead. These defeats, especially Poitiers, were humiliating and decisive defeats for the French, whose political landscape was greatly affected by them. Still, while the English were able to secure favorable terms and either reinforce historical claims or gain more land on the French coast, they were not powerful enough to move into the heartland of France to fully conquer the country and claim the French throne outright.

Fifty-nine years later, in 1415, the French and English were still at war, though they had maintained an uneasy and frequently broken peace for a number of decades after Poitiers. The young warrior Henry V, of Shakespearean fame, was on the throne of England at this time. He and his "band of brothers" were in France to reinforce their claim on the French throne through Henry's great-grandfather, Edward III. Henry had only come to the throne of England two years earlier and was challenged in his rule and power from many different quarters. Asserting his claim in France and winning a military victory would go a long way to cementing his power. Though Henry was fully prepared to go to war, he was also prepared to negotiate with the French for much less than the French throne—he wanted official French acknowledgment of English claims on Aquitaine and a number of other smaller coastal French areas, especially major port cities.

Already having been humiliated enough by the English, the French refused Henry's terms, and the war was on again. This time, as you may know from Kenneth Branagh's *Henry V* (1989) and the excellent 2019 movie *The King*, the French were defeated once more, this time at Agincourt. Of the estimated 6,000 French dead, most were members of the nobility, which further weakened the French kingdom. As part of the peace terms, Henry (who had lost only 600 men) married the youngest daughter of the French king, further complicating already complicated matters of blood, inheritance, and rule.

Still, despite another decisive English victory on the battlefield, Henry was not strong enough to push his claim to the French throne and still remain strong in England, where plots and the Scottish always threatened his power. The war went on, but the tide was about to turn.

The Maid of Orléans

Three years before the English victory at Agincourt, a farmer's daughter was born in the town of Domrémy in the Vosges Mountains of northeastern France. Her father's name was Jacques d'Arc. So, contrary to what some people might think, Joan of Arc was not born in a town called "Arc." The area where Joan was born was caught in between French factions, or rather between the people loyal to the royal family of France and those loyal to the ruling families of the Duchy of Burgundy, which, you can see from the map at the end of the last chapter, retained its independence, had its own claims on the French throne, and was allied with the English.

Joan, like many children in Europe at the time, was no stranger to war. Raids and skirmishes between local lords and between forces loyal to one side and another occurred throughout the area. At one point, her father's farm was burned to the ground.

At about the age of thirteen, Joan reported she had religious visions and heard voices. In her first vision, she saw three figures that she believed were Archangel Michael and the early Christian martyrs and saints Catherine and Margaret. According to Joan's later testimony, these three figures instructed her to drive the English out of France and to support Charles VII of France, the eldest son of Charles VI, who had yet to be crowned.

Historians have debated the nature of Joan's visions. Many believe they were true religious revelations, although this was more so in the past than today. However, hundreds of thousands, if not millions, of Frenchmen and women and many other Catholics still adhere to the idea that Joan was "touched by God." More recently, historians, psychologists, and others believe that Joan may have suffered from schizophrenia, a type of migraine, or epilepsy. Others have posited that she ingested a type of mold known as "ergot" that infects rye grain. Ergot poisoning has been known to cause hallucinations. Some have also put forth the theory that Joan acquired bovine tuberculosis, which can affect the brain, from drinking unpasteurized milk (obviously, since "pasteurization" was developed in the 19th century by famed French scientist Louis Pasteur, all milk prior to this was "unpasteurized" and could possibly lead to some type of sickness). However, if Joan had been sick with this type of tuberculosis, she would not have been able to become the active person she was destined to be.

Whatever the cause of Joan's visions, they were real enough for her to believe and act on. One does not go from peasant girl to hero of the nation unless they are convinced something monumental has happened. Between the ages of thirteen and sixteen, Joan, who referred to herself as Jeanne la Pucelle ("Joan the Maid"), had a number of these religious experiences. At the age of sixteen, she asked a male relative to escort her to the nearest royalist military garrison, where she appeared in front of the post's commander and asked to be taken to the court of the king, some 200 miles away. As you can imagine, she was dismissed with laughter, but a few months later, she returned and spoke with two of the commander's men and convinced them she was telling the truth. These two officers took her once again to the post commander, where she repeated her story about the visions that approached her and predicted that the French and their Scottish allies were about to lose a battle to the English near Orléans. A few days later, word arrived at the post that just such a defeat had happened.

Having already told the commander, a minor noble named Robert de Baudricourt, about her visions and now having told him that she had seen the battle's outcome while tending her fields, he offered to take her to Chinon to see the Dauphin. The eldest son of the French king was called the Dauphin as he had not yet been crowned king; father and son had fought each other, leading to the French court being divided by factions.

Arriving in Chinon, Joan met with Charles and told him of her visions and the voices guiding her to her destiny. Charles VII's father was a man who was mentally ill and reportedly believed at times that he was made of glass and about to break into a thousand pieces at any moment. He had also reported seeing visions or hallucinations, so the young prince was used to people making and acting upon unusual claims. As far as we know, Charles VII and Joan's meeting went so well that she was able to convince him that her appearance at the continuing siege of Orléans would lead to a French victory over the English.

Contrary to Hollywood legend, Joan did not take part in hand-to-hand combat at Orléans or anywhere else for that matter, though she was twice wounded—once by an arrow and once by a crossbow bolt. Joan's role in the siege was to inspire the troops. Backed by the Dauphin, she told her story to the troops and their leaders, wore armor given to her by Charles, and urged the French soldiers on during the battle, convincing them that God had already given them the victory.

Orléans was and still is a major city in the heart of France, 85 miles south of Paris and just over 250 miles from the English Channel. It sits upon the Loire River, one of the key commercial rivers in France then and today. Control of Orléans would give the English a significant advantage over the French in the fight for control of the country.

By the time Joan arrived at Orléans, the English had been there for five months fighting off the French siege, which was seemingly going nowhere. However, at the time of Joan's arrival, the battle had begun to swing in favor of the French, with provincial French troops seizing a number of smaller strongpoints around the city and keeping the English bottled up within.

On May 7th, 1428, Joan, who was dressed in battle armor, arrived on the front lines during the battle for the main British strongpoint. Word of Joan's visions and her confidence that God and his angels were on the side of the French had encouraged the French troops, so her arrival at the scene of combat spurred the French on. It seems that Joan, by waving her banner, which depicted Christ and his angels as well as the symbol of French royalty, the fleur-de-lys, and encouraging the soldiers with assurances that God was watching, may have turned the tide of battle that day. It was then that she took an English arrow between the neck and shoulders. She was taken from the frontlines, treated, and then returned to the area of the fighting to drive the men forward in their final assault on the English position. The English were forced to retreat from Orléans after the capture of their main strongpoint.

Illustration 16: Joan's pennon/banner, based on historical descriptions.

Illustration 17: Image of Joan from a 1429 French document, though the artist never saw Joan personally. In the Romantic Era of the 19th century, Joan was a much-painted figure, but virtually all of those paintings/sculptures are inaccurate.

Before the battle, Joan had promised a sign from God to the French. The victory at Orléans was taken to be that sign, and Joan was elevated to a position of greater influence. Her suggestions for a French attack on the far-off English-held city of Rouen were accepted. Over the course of the next month and a half, Joan and others led the French to a series of astounding victories over the English. Joan was wounded again but again recovered, which was taken as a further sign of God's approval.

On July 16th, 1429, the city of Reims, where French kings were traditionally crowned and blessed, was taken bloodlessly by the French, and Charles VII was officially made the king of France. Joan and the French army then moved toward Paris, which had been occupied by the English for some time, taking a number of towns outside of the city and threatening the English positions. These battles and skirmishes took place in the fall and winter of 1429, which was when Joan was struck by the aforementioned crossbow bolt in the thigh. For her sacrifices and her role in leading the French, Joan and her family were given noble titles. This was the high point of her life, for the rest of it was short and destined to end in the most medieval fashion possible.

Joan had made the war with the English into a sort of holy crusade with her stories of visions and predictions. Of course, in every religious war, there are two sides whose views are interchangeable, depending on who you're talking about or to. In a time when nearly everyone was devoutly religious, those who opposed you were on the side of the devil, and this is how the English saw Joan; to them, she was an agent of Satan.

In the winter and early spring of 1430, the French and English upheld an uneasy truce, but when the weather improved, the fighting began again. On May 23rd, 1430, Joan was with a group of French soldiers attempting to break the English siege of Compiègne, which is north of Paris. (As an interesting side note, this city would play a significant role in the 20th century as the place where the Germans surrendered to the French in WWI and where Hitler forced the French to capitulate to him in 1940.)

Joan and her column of horsemen were ambushed by Burgundians, who were allied with the English. Joan was dragged from her horse and captured. Joan was clearly a charismatic person, and she was also obviously quite brave. In addition to her wounds in battle, she attempted to escape captivity, including once when she jumped some seventy feet out of the tower in which she was held. Luckily, she landed on very soft earth and was relatively unharmed, but she was recaptured.

The English prevailed upon the Burgundians to release Joan to them, which they did so for a price. She was taken to the city of Rouen, halfway between Paris and the English Channel on the Seine River, which was the base of English operations in France. Joan was held there for a year, during which the French attempted a number of abortive rescue attempts. Of course, she was also famously put on trial for heresy.

Heresy, as defined by the Oxford English Dictionary, is "belief or opinion contrary to orthodox religious (especially Christian) doctrine." Of course, the English at the time were Catholic, just like the French, but they wished to prove that Joan was lying about her visions and claiming to "speak for God," which they claimed was a heretical act. Other charges were brought against her, including the very serious charge of dressing like a man. She had done this in battle and in prison, as she had refused to give up her clothes. She felt that pants were more of an obstacle to remove than the simple shift they tried to get her to wear, and she knew that rape was a very real possibility. In other words, the English were trying to do what most accusers do even to this day—throw mud against the wall and see what sticks. At the time, a woman dressing as a man or attempting to pass as a man was a serious offense. Her famous "bobbed" hairstyle, which was similar to that worn by the French king and French soldiers, for both reasons of cleanliness and combat, was also used to accuse her of passing as a man. This was key for the charge of heresy, which was only punishable by death the second time someone was accused. However, when the cross-dressing charge was added, Joan was in real danger.

Her trial was conducted by French and Burgundian clergy who were clearly pro-English, either because they were on the English payroll or were allied with them. English soldiers at the trial were there not only to prevent Joan from being rescued but also to act as an unspoken threat to anyone who voted against punishing Joan.

During the trial, Joan stunned the court with her intelligence, despite the fact that she was illiterate and had no formal education. The trial was recorded for posterity, though many of Joan's statements were altered in the final document. At the end of the trial, Joan was ordered to sign a document, the contents of which she could not possibly know and which she could not sign without help since she could not write. The order was given under threat of death, and Joan signed a document stating that she had never had the visions that she claimed to have had. She also forswore wearing men's clothes. A few days later, Joan changed back into men's clothes while in prison (she had reported rape attempts before the trial). This was clearly a trap and one which was designed to catch her going back on her "signed and sworn testimony before God." A death sentence was pronounced, and on May 30th, 1431, she was burned at the stake in the center of Rouen. The English burned her body again to prevent anyone from getting her bones, as relics of holy or revered figures were important aspects of life in medieval Christendom. Her ashes were dumped in the Seine River. Joan was nineteen at the time of her death.

The Hundred Years' War continued for another twenty-odd years after the death of Joan. The ascension of Henry VI of England, who was a weak king, enabled the French to gain the upper hand and drive the English out of most of France, save a small number of coastal cities on the Channel.

In 1920, Pope Benedict XV canonized Joan, but by that time, she was already a sainted figure in France. Charles VII had also ordered a new investigation and trial of Joan in the 1450s, which, of course, cleared her of all the charges that had been levied against her. To this day, Joan of Arc's spirit has been invoked by the French in times of war and hardship. Statues, mostly Romantic Era creations, showing Joan charging into battle abound throughout the country, especially in Orléans and the other cities that played an important role in her life. There are also numerous statues of Joan in the USA, including in the nation's capital.

Illustration 18: Statue of Joan in Orléans, France.

Chapter 7 – "L'état, c'est moi" ("I am the state")

"I am the state," declared Louis XIV (1638-1715). Louis XIV was the absolute king of France and one of the most interesting figures in French history. He reigned over France from 1643 to 1715, and during that time, he fashioned France into the most powerful nation in Europe. Louis, for reasons that will be explained, also was the epitome of the phrase "absolute monarch," and many historians consider his reign to be a distant forerunner of the authoritarian regimes of the 20th century.

Due to his power and immense personality, Louis also became *the* trendsetter in Europe. His fashion, his taste, and especially his palace all became the templates for contemporary and later kings and queens, not only in France but also throughout Europe. The most famous portrait of Louis XIV, which was done by Hyacinthe (a French corruption of his Catalan name of Jacint) Rigaud in 1701, shows the aging king resplendent in purple (the color of royalty since the days of the Roman Empire) and white ermine robes, wearing his famous black curly wig, light blue hose with gold high-heel shoes, a broadsword, and his crown and scepter.

Today, Louis might be viewed as a dandified and effeminate figure of ridicule. But then? Louis XIV was the absolute epitome of manhood. In his younger life, he was a notorious womanizer, and he engaged with an innumerable number of concubines, some of whom grew quite rich and influential at his court. Louis was also trained in the art of war, and though his armies were often defeated, he was a capable military leader and also knew how to delegate to his commanders. Lastly, Louis XIV could be absolutely ruthless. Many of his enemies met the ultimate fate, many times suffering the pains of torture before being killed. Anyone questioning Louis's manhood would likely have met a similar fate.

Before we delve into Louis's life, let's quickly examine the centuries between the death of Joan of Arc and the rise of Louis XIV.

It is difficult to review in just a few paragraphs the monumental changes that occurred in Europe from the time about fifty years before the birth of St. Joan to the ascension of Louis XIV, but for our purposes here, three historical eras or events concern us: the

Renaissance, the Protestant Reformation/St. Bartholomew's Day massacre, and the weakening of the French monarchy before Louis XIV.

The Renaissance, or "Rebirth," refers to the revival of and building upon Greek and Roman ideas in Europe. There is no single date that one can look back on and say, "On this day, the Renaissance began." Rather, it was a gradual process that had actually been taking place quietly for decades before its explosion in the mid-1300s.

There are a number of factors that caused this explosion of study, knowledge, and scientific and cultural reflowering. Among them was the rediscovery of Greek and Roman writings that had long been secured in Christian monasteries and Muslim libraries. In the case of the former, many Greek and Roman writings and ideas lay discarded, remnants of a time when the Catholic Church was still, in many ways, a very "Roman" institution and its doctrine still in flux.

The solidification of Catholic doctrine in the centuries after the fall of the Roman Empire, at a time when authority was generally unquestioned (often because of an illiterate/uneducated populace), meant that whatever did not agree with official church teachings was either forbidden or literally stored and hidden away. The monasteries, which were isolated communities of relatively learned men, were the places where these documents and ideas were stored, sometimes literally in the hopes of more educated times.

Islam, which rose from the sands of Arabia in the 700s and spread rapidly through the Middle East and into Spain, did not become the scientifically stagnant entity that European Christendom became. It's interesting that just as Europe was beginning to experience the beginnings of people questioning religious dogma, much of the Islamic world was heading in the opposite direction. However, in the years between the rise of Islam and the Renaissance, the Islamic world safeguarded many of the great works of the Romans and Greeks, both of whom had great direct or indirect influence in the Middle East and North Africa. While Europe descended into the Dark Ages of ignorance, Muslim scholars rediscovered or built upon the ideas of Plato, Aristotle, and Hippocrates, as well as many of the Roman histories and other works, especially in the realm of architecture and art.

During the 600-odd years of medieval Europe, much trade (along with much war) went on between Europe and the Islamic world, especially that of Muslim Spain. Ideas and sometimes documents were not the only things brought back from the Islamic world, as tales of the amazing architecture and gardens of the caliphs and other Muslim leaders were too. These buildings and sometimes even the gardens were built on mathematical principles discovered by the Greeks, which were then used by the Romans and elaborated upon by the Muslims.

This exposure to ancient and new ideas also led to a rediscovery of the works that were essentially hidden in plain sight in monasteries throughout Europe, especially in the home of the former Roman Empire, the lands of Italy, where the Renaissance can be said to have started. By the time Louis XIV became king in his own right in 1661, after eighteen years of a regency that held power in his stead, Europe had been experiencing a period of scientific and artistic growth that it had not witnessed in more than a thousand years.

This period of cultural and scientific learning had its limits, as it began to encroach on both church power and beliefs. In the years before 1517, before German priest Martin Luther nailed his *Ninety-five Theses* (charges leveled against the Catholic Church of its more questionable practices) to the church door in Wittenberg and began the Protestant Reformation, the Catholic Church had become the dominant feature not only of the Continent's spiritual life but also of its economic, legal, and moral life as well. Anything that went against the beliefs and practices of the church (unless, of course, you were rich and powerful) was liable to be deemed "heresy" and punished severely, as you have seen with Joan of Arc in the prior chapter.

The most famous example of these types of restrictions is the famous case of Galileo Galilei, the Italian astronomer who challenged church beliefs by stating that the earth revolved around the sun, implying that the planet was not the center of God's universe. Galileo's fame and the retraction of his beliefs under threat saved him from being burned at the stake, but it sent a clear message that the church would only put up with so many challenges to its authority.

However, that could only be the case if it was powerful enough to hold the challenges back. Over the centuries, the people of Europe had watched the Catholic Church grow incredibly rich and powerful, all while telling the populace that one sure way of getting to heaven was through the humility that came with poverty. The tipping point for Martin Luther came when he witnessed many of his fellow clergy selling indulgences. Simply put, these were payments made to the church (or a particular churchman) in order to secure one's place in heaven. Essentially, people were buying their way out of sin by "donating" to the church. Of course, this practice had no root in Christian theology, but no one, except for Luther and a few others, was willing to risk their life in challenging the practice.

Luther and the people had also seen priests and monks be married and have concubines and children when the Catholic clergy had been sworn to celibacy since the 11th century. Of course, God only knows the extent of the sexual abuses that must have occurred in the church at a time before any kind of press or free speech. This most likely only added to the resentment felt by the people of Europe.

You can read more about the Protestant Reformation in Captivating History's *The Reformation*, as well as in thousands upon thousands of other books, papers, and articles, but for our purposes here, suffice it to say that by the time of Louis XIV, the Reformation had split western and central Europe into two Christian belief systems, which warred with each other figuratively and literally throughout the 16th and 17th centuries (as a side note, there was a third branch, that of Orthodox Christianity, which primarily remained in the Balkans and Russia). These wars were not limited to national borders—they often took place within nations. The Thirty Years' War took more lives within Germany than it did outside the country, and to this day, Germany is more heavily Protestant in the north of the country and more Catholic in the south.

France was not immune to this religious strife, and one event more than any other illustrates the struggle for religious freedom in the country. This event and those surrounding it may have led to Louis XIV making the greatest decision of his reign, which affected not only France but also set off a chain of events that led to the settlements in the New World and the amazing flowering of freedom and inquiry known as the Enlightenment. These later events, in turn, led directly to the American Revolution, the French Revolution, and the modern world as we know it today.

In France, the Protestant Revolution found some limited success, but, as opposed to the lands of Germany and Italy, the country was not fractured into many different states with its own kings and independent rulers. Thus, the Catholic Church and the monarchy of France were able to more greatly control the effects of the Reformation in the country, with a couple of small exceptions. One of them was the relatively independent Kingdom of Navarre, a small entity in the southwest of France on the Spanish border. In 1572, the king of Navarre was Henry III, who was Protestant and also had a claim to the French throne. His ascension to the French throne is confusing even to professional historians, but suffice it to say that Henry overcame all other claims to the throne, and through his marriage to the impressive Margaret of Valois, he became the king of France, taking the name of Henry IV, in August 1589. However, to take the throne, he was required to do one thing: convert to Catholicism. Henry famously proclaimed, "France is worth a mass."

However, many Frenchmen and women were not convinced his conversion was real, so they harbored great enmity toward any French Protestant, which was returned in kind. Of course, there was criticism to Henry's right to the throne. This culminated in the Saint Bartholomew's Day massacre, which occurred a few days after Henry's marriage to Margaret of Valois in August 1572 (it also coincides with that saint's day). This massacre included the assassinations of some of Henry's friends and allies (mainly Protestants), an attempt on the king's life, and the wholesale slaughter of Protestants, first in Paris and then throughout the country. Modern estimates of the dead number from 10,000 to 40,000. Prior to the massacre and the battles that followed it, the French Protestant population is estimated to have been around 10 percent. Afterward, the estimates sit at around 6 percent.

Henry survived the massacre, and as king, he did his best to quell religious warfare in France with his Edict of Nantes in 1598, which attempted to legalize religious tolerance within his kingdom, give Protestants the right to practice their religious beliefs freely, and remove a number of economic sanctions. But throughout the last part of the 1500s and into the 1600s, France was wracked by not only religious civil wars but also a breakdown of royal authority, with church figures dominating weak kings and with nobles fighting each other for the right to claim the throne, which was not also religious in nature. Among the victims of this strife was Henry IV, who was assassinated in 1610 by a fanatic Catholic. He was Louis XIV's grandfather. Louis XIV was born into this situation in 1638. He was the son of Louis XIII, called Louis the Just. He reigned for thirty-three years, but his rule was marred by palace intrigue, plots, and his inability to rule on his own. Famously, he turned to Cardinal Richelieu, who was depicted in *The Three Musketeers*, to govern the country in his later years. Though one of Louis the Just's accomplishments was to declare that the monarchy, rather than the nobles of the country, had the right to the ultimate use of force, the aristocrats continued to struggle with each other for riches and power, with some plotting to take the throne themselves.

Though Louis XIV was only a boy when his father died, the struggles inside the palace and for power among the nobles left a strong impression on him. When his father died, Louis was only four years old. Despite the last wishes of his father, Louis's mother, Anne of Austria, seized power as the regent, along with her adviser and the former king's right-hand man Cardinal Richelieu. Though Louis was officially the king, he would not have power until he took it for himself at the age of twenty-three in 1661.

Throughout his teens, Louis was given increasing responsibility and was instructed in the arts and sciences that he would need when he became king in his own right, such as warfare, fencing, math, economics, religion, and the classics of Rome and Greece. As he grew older, he chafed against the rule of his mother and Richelieu's successor, Cardinal Mazarin. One incident, in particular, may have determined Louis's later course to take all the power unto himself.

In 1648, a series of uprisings against royal power, collectively known as the Fronde (for the slings used by peasants during the riots), erupted. The main conflict came between the monarchy and the Parlement, a body of nobles and clergy who were eager to seize more power. They were especially eager to bring down Anne of Austria and Cardinal Mazarin, who was Italian, as they were seen as foreign interlopers attempting not only to seize complete power in France but also place her under the thumb of foreign powers.

The Fronde turned quite violent, and at one point, a mob went to the royal palace on rumors that Louis XIV had been killed by those loyal to Anne in an attempt to place her on the throne. The mob marched into the palace, demanding to see the king and threatening to kill anyone who stood in the way. In the middle of the night, they barged into Louis XIV's bedchamber, where he lay in bed, feigning sleep. Satisfied that the king was alive, the mob left. Louis awoke, vowing that when he took power, France would never fall into the hands of a mob again. The Fronde, as well as the Second Fronde, which took place from 1650 to 1653, were put down by Anne and Mazarin.

Rumors of Anne's hunger for personal power were untrue, as her later life's work was dedicated to Louis becoming the unquestioned king of France. When Mazarin died in the spring of 1661, Louis became king in his own right. His first act as king was to abolish the role of chief minister, the position held by Mazarin and Richelieu, instead taking the rule all for himself. When he announced his intention to the court, Louis left no doubt that France was embarking on a new era: "You will assist me with your counsels when I ask for them...You will seal no orders except by my command...I order you to not sign anything, not even a passport without my command...[You will] render account to me each day."

It is hard to overemphasize the effect of Louis's personality on the royal court and on the nation itself. He soon declared himself to be *le Roi Soleil*, the "Sun King," a figure who illuminates France and whom France revolves around. This may be a hard idea to understand in the 21st century, and indeed many French nobles at the time, who were accustomed to ruling almost as virtual kings themselves, chafed at Louis's ideas of power. However, behind Louis's grandiosity was the idea of the divine right of kings, an idea that was not at all unique to France.

Simply put, this divine right is that God, who rules over all things, has a divine plan. Since this was a time of virtually unquestioned religious devotion, people believed that it must be true that God put the king on the throne. And since God himself ordained the kingship, the king was obviously the representative of God on Earth. And, according to Louis XIV, one does not disobey God.

As if that was not enough, the king was essentially considered to be two entities: the person of the king—the man—and the embodiment of France as ordained by God. Louis XIV grasped those ideas, built upon them, and never let them go.

France at the Time of Louis XIV

When Louis became king in his own right, he oversaw a kingdom that was both rich and powerful, and he was determined to increase this wealth and influence. Like the English, Spanish, Portuguese, and Dutch, the French had embarked on voyages of discovery and colonization. Though the French acquired territory and trading rights in various places in the Far East and India, its push for an empire was mainly focused on the Caribbean and North America, where they came into conflict with the British. The major wars between England and France would be something that Louis's successors would have to deal with, but during his reign, Louis not only had his forces occasionally fighting the British in the New World (mainly but not exclusively in the Caribbean and at sea) but also in Europe. Louis engaged in a series of wars (sometimes alongside his ally Catholic Spain, which was the home of his first wife, Maria Theresa) against the Protestant powers of England, Holland, and many of the northern German states. For Louis, who was a devout Catholic despite his incredible womanizing, these wars were both his religious duty and his responsibility to keep France safe and prosperous. In Europe, his main aim was to enlarge the French nation to the north and east, creating a buffer zone between his kingdom and the Protestants, and to seize (or indirectly control) the smaller duchies, baronies, and principalities that made up most of the area bordering eastern France.

Of course, there was one last reason: to glorify himself. Louis was not above going to the frontlines and directing the battle or at least advising his generals. He was brave and was often in range of enemy guns and cannons. The fact that he was never injured added to his own ideas of his superiority and God's favor.

In the end, however, along with Louis's lavish spending on his own court and palace, the wars he began would eventually contribute to the dire economic straits faced by Louis's great-great-great-grandson, Louis XVI, in 1789, the time of the French Revolution. Louis XIV's wars and the wars of his successors eventually ended in defeat, with some exceptions, and resulted in the rise of England as the preeminent power in the world.

However, in 1661, when Louis fully came to the throne, that was all in the future. During Louis's reign, France became one of the richest nations in the world, and Louis was determined to let everyone know it.

Illustration 19: Symbol of Louis as the Sun King, featured on the main gate to the Palace of Versailles.

Louis's Personality

Today, we would undoubtedly classify Louis XIV as an egomaniac, possibly a megalomaniac. What you are about to read will sound incredibly strange, and it was, but for those who lived at the time, especially those in the upper classes of France and especially at the royal court at Versailles, it was everyday "normal" life. The rituals developed by the king were, for the most part, followed to the letter, at least when he was at the palace. Sometimes these rituals and Louis's own need to be constantly on display as both the king and God's representative of France weighed on him, and he would, so to speak, "let his hair down" at a smaller residence on the Versailles grounds, one of the other royal palaces, or among intimates, both his lovers and those who under normal circumstances might be called friends.

Illustration 20: Aerial view of Versailles today. In Louis's time, the town itself was much smaller and the grounds of the palace larger. There are some 700 rooms in the main building.

Louis developed a curious and brilliant way to maintain control of the French nobles, which was necessary. For many decades before Louis's ascension to the throne, an assortment of nobles had been either attempting to gain the throne of France for themselves or had been trying to weaken the power of the king and gain more control for themselves. Louis had grown up in tumultuous times and was determined that he would be the ultimate power in France. To this end, he forced (mostly in a nice, polite but unmistakably commanding way) many nobles to live at the court of Versailles.

For some nobility, especially as Louis's power and the grandeur of the palace grew, this was an honor. Many became Louis's confidantes or members of his inner circle. This honor was limited to powerful nobles and clergymen. Other nobles, especially if they were from areas far from Versailles or from restive provinces, were asked to take up residence at the court for a time so Louis could keep an eye on them. In the 1660s, the royal court of Louis XIV numbered some 600 to 700 people. Toward the end of Louis's reign, this number was closer to ten thousand. Oftentimes, their daughters gladly offered themselves up to the king, who was a notorious womanizer in his younger and middle years. In many cases, family members were more than happy that the king began to "see" their female relatives, as this brought positive attention to their family and, many times, their pocketbooks, at least indirectly.

However, as time passed, life at the court and palace became ever grander and expensive. Guests were expected to dress accordingly, feed themselves (at least for the most part), and take part in the many ways to gamble at the court (an invitation to play cards or billiards with the king was perhaps the most sought-after invitation of them all). For many lesser nobles, a stay at Versailles, even for a couple of days, was enough to bankrupt them. In some cases, such a visit might cost half a person's lifetime savings or more. But that was part of the point. After all, who could one go to at the palace when they found themselves broke? There wasn't anyone else but the king. Thus, these nobles, many of whom had opposed the king in some way or other, became indebted to him. And, of course, we all know that once someone has you in their debt, they have you in their grasp.

Louis XIV accomplished much during his long reign, but Louis is perhaps best remembered for his palace and court at Versailles, which is open to all today, or at least most of it. By the time Louis XIV's great-great-great-grandson Louis XVI lost the throne of France in the early 1790s, over one-quarter of the expenditures of

France was spent on the palace. This included maintenance, further construction, and the expenses of the royal court. From the time of Louis XIV to Louis XVI, France was one of the richest countries on the planet, and a quarter of its expenditures were spent on the king's "house"!

The palace itself consists of some 700 rooms, some of them secret. The grounds are unbelievably elaborate, as you can see from the aerial picture on the prior page. The palace grounds feature perfectly geometric lawns and shrubbery, paths, incredible statues and fountains (some of which are both), and the Grand Canal, a semi-navigable waterway 1,670 meters in length. In addition to the grounds, smaller palaces and residences were built over the years, including smaller residences for the king, his wife, and his mistresses.

Within the palace itself are the famous Hall of Mirrors, which hosted not only the signing of the Treaty of Versailles that ended WWI but also the surrender of France in 1871, Louis's royal chapel, the private and public residences of the king and queen, an opera house, a theater, and an amazing number of salons and meeting rooms for various purposes.

Though each of the rooms at Versailles had a separate purpose, together with the grounds and the splendor of the court, they had one purpose: to overawe those visiting and in living there with Louis's power.

Illustration 21: The famous Hall of Mirrors. Much of the palace was destroyed or ruined during the French Revolution of 1789. Since that time, most of Versailles has been restored, with many of the original pieces returned to it.

Throughout the entire palace, paintings and statues portrayed Louis in various roles, such as the king, the intermediary between God and man, the reincarnation of the Greek sun-king Apollo, a knight and/or general, a family man, the father to the country, and much else. Looking about the palace through today's eyes, it is easy to see that Louis was an egomaniac of a scale seldom seen in the world, and in many cases, it is easy to shake one's head or laugh at the scale of his self-centeredness. But one must remember Louis XIV wasn't a king in the 21st century. He was a king in the 17th and 18th centuries, and times were much different. Louis and most of the people of France (both noble and otherwise) believed he was placed on the throne by God himself. Not only did they believe that, but they also believed that Louis was not only Louis but the embodiment of France. A noble or commoner coming into contact with Louis for the first time must have been absolutely overwhelmed.

What is amazing about this is that, by all accounts, Louis could at times (usually behind closed doors) be amazingly personable and real. For the most part, when Louis was with his advisers debating matters of state, he tolerated dissent from his own opinion as long as it was tempered and not overly familiar. Louis was not a stupid, vain man. He was educated in the arts, military affairs, math, science, and much else. He was able to keep up with the most learned men of his day, or at least to the point of being able to ask them important questions, and he allowed artists, scientists, and ministers to disagree with him, even encouraging them to do so. However, there was a limit. If Louis's mind was made up and he gave a command or a strongly worded "suggestion," it had to be followed.

Louis had a small residence built near the town of Marly, which is not far from Versailles. Today, the town is known as Marly-le-Roi ("Marly of the King"). Here, Louis would relax, sometimes even greeting visitors in a bathrobe and skullcap. Louis's hair had fallen out as a young man, and to compensate for this, he began wearing the elaborate wigs for which we know him. It became the fashion, not only in France but also throughout the Western world. These times at Marly were welcome and rare for Louis, for he trapped himself in a world of daily rituals that were followed to the letter at Versailles.

Every day the king was in residence at Versailles and even, with some variation, when he was on campaign with his armies, a strict ritual was followed. The king would be awoken every morning at the same time. While he roused himself, his chamber pot from the night before would be removed and given to his personal physician and his staff. They would examine the king's urine and stool closely, monitoring any change from the days or weeks before. In one case, blood in the king's stool led to the discovery of a fistula in his colon. The king underwent a painful and life-saving operation while conscious.

Once the king had risen from his bed, a retinue of servants and nobles would enter his apartment. Each was assigned a task, whether it was to put on the king's robe or to help with his slippers. Those most in favor with the king attended to these "events." For example, if someone had been the person to hand the king his hat as he left the apartment for some time and then told to hold open the door for the king after he had dressed, that was not a good sign. In that instance, the king and/or his closest advisers had determined that someone else was more important or that this person had displeased the king in some way.

The king often took breakfast and lunch with his intimates or closest advisers, but dinner was a public affair. The king sat at the center of a long table, with his closest relatives and favorites down on either side of him, facing outward. They were not alone. Before the king's table was a small gallery with seating, where nobles and other important personages (artists, mistresses, clergy, wives of nobles, etc.) would sit or stand to watch the king eat. Each course was announced as it was brought to the table. Louis would partake of each dish before anyone else touched it. Once he had eaten what he wanted (he rarely filled up on one dish as there were many to come), that dish was passed to those at the table in order of importance and/or rank. This could go on for literally hours. As one can imagine, seats in the front row meant you were in the king's favor. If you were a "nobody" from the provinces (that is, a baron from miles and miles away), you might bribe a court official for a place to stand during the meal and hope that you somehow caught the king's eye.

If one managed to do that, you might be told to attend the king's promenade, which was Louis's regular walk around the main palace grounds. Of course, the king and the royal family would lead. They would be followed by his advisers, priests, generals in attendance, and so on in importance. They would then be followed by a myriad of minor nobility, some of whom lived at the palace (at least temporarily) and some of whom were visiting. Oftentimes before the royal walk, Louis would be informed of who was in attendance at the palace, and he would decide who joined him. If someone had displeased the king in some way, he might tell those in charge of the walk, "I have never heard of that person." That was a sign that whoever the king was speaking about was in hot water, and it was often a message to that person that the king expected them to change their ways or opinion, to offer the king a gift, or to simply go away. When Louis's coterie joined him for the walk, everyone knew who was where. Any absence or movement toward the rear or closer to the king was noted, as one's well-being might depend on it.

Versailles was the crown jewel of Louis XIV's realm, and it was the symbol of France's power and influence. It was at this time that French really became *the* language of diplomacy, reflecting not only France's power but also its style, culture, and influence. If you are interested in learning more about Versailles, you will find references to a video and website on the building and glory of Versailles, as well as on the life of Louis XIV, at the end of this book. However, Versailles is just part of Louis's story.

For much of Louis's reign, France's economy was healthy. He reorganized the country's tax system and expanded it to increase revenue. The government (meaning Louis) had a monopoly on the mining, cultivation, and sale of salt, which was needed for the curing of meat in a time with no refrigeration, and it also had a monopoly on the creation and sale of matches, which was, again, a needed commodity before gas and electric lighting and heating. On all of the major roads of France, there were tolls. In most instances, these were controlled by a local lord who paid Louis for the right to do so. Everyone expected the locals to take a cut above what they reported collecting, but as long as Louis saw his share, he found it acceptable.

Additionally, France's income rose from increased trade around the world. France imported fine goods, such as porcelain, jewels, and spices, as well as exported them, mainly doing so in the form of textiles. Much of Louis's reign saw good harvests, and in general, most of the people were happy or at least satisfied with Louis's rule.

One group of people who were not at all happy with the rule of Louis XIV were the Protestants of France. As you read earlier, Louis's ancestor, Henry IV, issued the Edict of Nantes in 1598, which gave religious liberty to Protestants who had been severely persecuted, killed, and forced to hold their services in secret or renounce their religion. Henry adopted Catholicism in order to ascend the throne, and though he was a relatively popular king with many achievements to his name, he was assassinated in 1610 by a Catholic fanatic who believed his conversion was disingenuous.

Louis XIV was a devout Catholic and attended Mass frequently. His chapel at Versailles was constructed under his direct instruction and is one of the more beautiful areas of the palace. The king even had a small chapel installed behind a secret wall in one of his apartments so he could worship, pray, and meditate unobserved.

Many reasons have been put forward for Louis XIV's revocation of the Edict of Nantes in 1685. By that time, Louis had been in sole charge of the kingdom for twenty-four years. During that time, he had engaged in numerous wars, put down rebellions, and had many of those opposed to him tortured and/or killed. He also slept with countless women and had many children by them, all while being married to his first wife, Maria Theresa of Spain. Louis also spent much of his energy gathering all of the power in the country around himself and worked tirelessly for what he believed was the "unity" of the country. After all, as you have read, his younger years were somewhat chaotic. A number of historians believe Louis's revocation of the Edict of Nantes was a way for him to atone for his many sins. Many also believe that the revocation was a way for

Louis to further his aim of unifying France under one God and one king, who was God's instrument on Earth.

So, on October 18th, 1685, Louis formally revoked the Edict of Nantes and took away all legal protections of Protestants in France. He also instituted a policy that became known as the Dragonnards, which had dragoons (cavalry units) move into Protestant areas, mostly in the southwestern parts of the country, where they were quartered among the families there. These families were responsible for feeding and housing them. Since Protestants no longer enjoyed protection under the law, all kinds of abuse went on, though Louis supposedly forbade the worse types of it, meaning rape and torture. Protestants were also forcibly made to attend Catholic Mass and lectures given by priests or bishops on the evils of Protestantism and the glory of the Catholic Church. At some point, Protestants were made to publicly make an abjuration, a public renunciation of Protestant teachings and acceptance of Catholicism.

Needless to say, many Protestants were killed and abused during this period. In some cases, there were armed uprisings, but these were put down ruthlessly and did not amount to much. Many Protestants abjured, some of them truthfully, as they were convinced that might did indeed make right. Others publicly followed Catholic practice but privately remained Protestant. This could be dangerous, for like the tyrants who followed in the 20th century, Louis knew that "educating" the children would have its uses. It would create new Catholics and spies in the household of many "former" Protestants, and many were indeed turned in by their children, sometimes on purpose and sometimes inadvertently.

The final result of the revocation of the edict was that France's Protestant population was reduced from about 10 percent to somewhere near 5 percent, and many fled the country. Some went to Holland, which had won its freedom from Spain in 1648, and others moved to England, where a form of Protestantism was the state religion. Others fled to Protestant German states, while still others decided to put a much greater distance between themselves by moving to the New World. Of these, many went to Canada, where France had colonies. They also moved to the English colonies in Canada and what would later become the United States.

The area under French control in Canada was called *Acadie*, or "Acadia," and it included what is now New Brunswick, Nova Scotia, and parts of Quebec. Forced from the regions by the Catholic majority, these Acadians fled as far as they could to another French colony, one more loosely controlled and with areas difficult to reach. This colony had been named Louisiana in honor of Louis XIV, and those Acadians slowly developed their own culture and French dialect. In time, the name *Acadien* became "Cajun." And this was all thanks to Louis XIV, at least indirectly.

At home, Louis XIV engaged in a number of wars throughout his reign. He succeeded in expanding French borders in the north to include all of present-day Belgium, and he pushed the influence of various German states back (Germany, as such, did not become a nation until 1871. Prior to that, what is now Germany was a collection of independent or semi-independent kingdoms, principalities, duchies, or bishoprics allied with various European rulers.) Louis saw to it that the states along France's eastern border were allied with him.

However, the other nations of western Europe, mainly England and Holland, were wary of every move that Louis made. France was then, as well as for many years, the largest and most populous nation in Europe, and the English and Dutch saw Louis's ego as an ever-present threat. For most of Louis's reign, France was involved in a war, whether it was large or small. To be a king in the 17th and 18th centuries was also to be a warlord. And one had to be a successful one, as no one respected a king who spent money on immense palaces and lost wars.

Toward the end of Louis's reign, his wars began to bankrupt the nation, along with his lavish expenditures. Worse still, a "grand coalition" had risen up against him in 1701 over questions of who would rise to the throne of Spain. Louis naturally wanted his grandson, Philip of Anjou, to be the Spanish king, and indeed, the dying king Charles (Carlos) II had named him as his successor.

Of course, the idea of Louis on the throne of France "guiding" his grandson in Spain was too much for England, Holland, the Holy Roman Empire, many German states (including the increasingly powerful Prussia), Portugal, and the powerful Italian state of Savoy. The rulers of the Holy Roman Empire were closely related to Louis, but even they knew that this move, which would allow Louis to influence Spanish policies, meant too much power in Louis's hands. The war raged on from 1701 to 1714, one year before Louis's death. One of the turning points of the war occurred in 1704 when Louis's armies were defeated at Blenheim, located northwest of Munich, Germany. Leading the English army was John Churchill, the soon-to-be-duke of Marlborough and the direct ancestor of Winston Churchill, who was born at Blenheim Palace (named for the great victory) in England in 1874.

The War of the Spanish Succession ended in 1714 with Philip on the throne of Spain, but he gave a solemn pledge to remain independent from France, which was enforced by a treaty. France did not lose territory, but it did lose prestige and treasure. England was the big "winner," as it secured the control of a number of ports around the world, trading rights, and the control of Gibraltar.

When Louis XIV died in 1715, France was on the path to bankruptcy. Good fortune would ebb and flow, but by the 1770s, French kings were borrowing huge sums of money to keep their kingdoms and their lavish lifestyles afloat. More wars and inept rulers would accelerate that process in the 1780s.

Louis was the king for seventy-two years—the longest of any monarch in recorded history. Louis XIV left behind Versailles. He also created the notion of an absolute monarchy, and some say he laid the groundwork for the modern "cult of personality" and police states of the 20th century. His crackdown on religious freedom and control of the arts led directly to the Enlightenment of the 1700s, which, in turn, led to both the American and French Revolutions.

Ten years before his death, Louis XIV commissioned wax sculptor Antoine Benoist to create a likeness of him. It is the only work of Benoist that has survived.

Chapter 8 – The French Revolution

Up to this point, we have been telling the story of France through some of its great personalities: Vercingetorix, Charlemagne, Joan of Arc, Louis XIV. For many years, a preponderance of historians believed that history was shaped by "great men" (and, at times, great women), who took control of destiny and shaped it to their own ends. That view of history is not as popular now as it used to be fifty years ago, but it serves as a good way to tell a story.

Perhaps in a time when kings and queens ruled and nobles and clergy vied for power, great men and women did make history, for the events of the life of everyday people were not recorded or even thought of as consequential. However, beginning in the early 18th century, history began to be made not so much by kings but by writers, thinkers, and the men in the street.

When Louis XIV died, his great-grandson, who became Louis XV, took power. Compared to Louis XIV, Louis XV was weak, corrupt, and relatively ineffectual. Although he was smart, he was shy and often let others speak for him. Like his famous grandson, Louis XVI, who followed him, Louis XV had a penchant for acting just a moment too late. He continued many of his great-grandfather's policies, including the suppression of Protestantism and increased government control of the arts. However, censorship of literature and art became a serious problem during Louis XV's reign.

Worse still, Louis XV had a reputation. Politely speaking, we would say he suffered from sex addiction. In truth, Louis slept with every woman he could, including many girls who had just "come of age." He infamously slept with two sisters, and his two most famous mistresses, Madame de Pompadour, whom he greatly loved, and Madame du Barry, were rumored to be the real powers in France. Madame du Barry was particularly hated by both the public and nobility for her lavish expenditures and supposed "power" over the king. She was beheaded during the French Revolution.

During his fifty-eight-year reign, Louis engaged in many wars, nearly all of them defeats, with some of them being outright disasters, like the Seven Years' War with England, which lost France most of its valuable possessions in the New World. These wars weakened not only France but also the king's reputation and France's finances.

As the French monarchy continued to grow weaker after the death of Louis XIV (who went unmourned for the most part after decades of rule as an autocratic father to the nation), more voices began to be heard criticizing the system. The period from about 1715 (the year Louis XIV died) to 1789 (the year the French Revolution began) is known as the Enlightenment, and while many men and women from around Europe and the American colonies began asserting rights and ideas previously unheard of or forbidden, it is France that is considered the home of the Enlightenment.

Perhaps some of the names of the great Enlightenment thinkers are familiar to you. They should be, as much of the bedrock of modern society, especially of Western democracy, was laid by them. Voltaire, Rousseau, Diderot, Montesquieu, and Buffon are some of the most known names, although there were dozens of other men and women, whether they were thinkers, artists, critics, writers, or politicians, who advanced the cause of human freedom after the death of Louis XIV.

Voltaire (1694–1778), who is credited with the famous saying, "I may not agree with you, but I will defend with my life your right to say it," led the way in the early part of the 18th century. Though this famous saying was a summation of Voltaire's beliefs uttered by a writer sometime after his death, the quote perfectly sums up the beliefs of the great Frenchman.

Voltaire, whose real name was François-Marie Arouet, grew famous from his writings, much of which criticized the French government, the Catholic clergy, and the nobility. This had to be done quite carefully in a hidden and subtle manner, for the regime of Louis XV, combined with the Catholic Church, censored any writing it believed was critical of it or of the Catholic faith. Voltaire was twice forced to flee France for England, where he saw for the first time a nation that enjoyed considerable individual freedoms, such as free speech and religion, which had been won at high cost in the 16th century during the English Civil War and afterward.

Voltaire was a prolific writer. He wrote hundreds of essays, poems, and letters addressing the problems of the day. His most famous work, *Candide,* was not so much a criticism of the French but rather the thinking of German philosopher Leibniz and the wave of relatively metaphysical ideas sweeping the upper and intellectual classes in Europe, the first and foremost one being that the world that exists at any one time must be the best one possible. For Voltaire, who throughout his life would attempt to open the eyes of his countrymen to the superstition and irrationality around them, this idea was simply playing into the hands of the powers that be—settling for your lot in life.

One of Voltaire's targets was the superstition of religion. Many people believe Voltaire was an atheist, but he was not. He believed that there *must* be a God, but that human beings, especially the Catholic Church, had added so much superstition, dogma, and unquestioning loyalty to it that they had perverted religion for their own purposes, mainly power and riches.

One of the most famous events in Voltaire's long life was the defense of Jean Calas, or rather the clearing of his name. Calas was a French Protestant who was accused of murdering his son because, it was believed, the son intended to convert to Catholicism. The trial of Calas was filled with injustice and unbelievable amounts of prejudice and superstition, and he was eventually convicted and tortured to death by authorities. Voltaire originally believing that Calas was guilty, but he looked into the case and found that Calas's son had committed suicide and that the trial was tainted by prejudice and religious intolerance. Though it was too late for Calas, Voltaire successfully argued the case in his writings, which by this time were followed by nearly the entire upper and intellectual classes of France, and he succeeded in having the sentence overturned posthumously. The family was paid a handsome amount by the king of France himself.

Jean-Jacques Rousseau (1712–1778) was born in Switzerland, but he spent most of his life in France. In contrast with Voltaire, who was known for his wit, charm, sophistication, and interest in a variety of subjects from religion to botany, Rousseau became focused early in his life on political philosophy and the injustices of society.

Though one is hesitant to use Wikipedia as a source, occasionally, there is something of great value there. In the article on Rousseau, one sentence sums up his life and two most famous works, *Discourse on Inequality* and *The Social Contract*. The entry reads, in part, "His [Rousseau's] *Discourse on Inequality* and *The*

Social Contract are the *cornerstones of modern political and social thought*" (author's italics).

It is exceedingly difficult to sum up Rousseau's works in a paragraph or two, but for our purposes here, suffice it to say that Rousseau believed that political authority came only in a social contract agreed upon by all the citizens in that society. Given free thought, it is unlikely that these citizens would vote for an aristocratic dictatorship or an absolute monarchy. All things being equal, they would likely push forward the idea of some sort of representative democracy. Most importantly, perhaps, Rousseau declared that the state of humankind was freedom. "Man is born free, but he is everywhere in chains." Of course, you can see how this might have influenced certain people by the names of Jefferson, Madison, Franklin, and Adams, and it most certainly did.

Alongside the writings and beliefs of Voltaire and Rousseau came a flowering of art and the beginnings of open political debate. All over France, the more liberal wealthy and increasingly numerous and influential middle classes gathered together in the salons of (usually) upper-class women, who were eager to show off both their connections and their knowledge. Since many of the *salonnières* of the time were women, they found themselves debating on equal footing the merits of one political or scientific idea or another with men.

Of course, most of the people were not titled aristocrats, famous writers, or of the middle class. Most of France was poor, and it had been poor since time immemorial. They did not have the time or luxury of debating one school of philosophical or scientific thought over another over tea (and, increasingly, coffee) in the salons of the rich and famous.

However, in the 1700s, the majority of people became more informed through the increasing growth of the newspaper. Though most people of the time were illiterate, a growing number, especially in cities like Paris, was learning how to read, and they would read the news of the day to their families and friends. Newspapers, which were really nothing more than pamphlets or broadsheets, began having loyal followings, and the vast majority of them were critical of one aspect or another, such as the church, the monarchy, or the aristocracy.

Of course, the popularity of the salons, the writings of the Enlightenment *philosophes*, and the newspapers brought about a backlash. Censorship was increased. Government spies were widespread in cities throughout the country, and many, including Voltaire, were jailed for their thoughts and opinions. In Paris, many of the "enemies of the King" were sent to the infamous Bastille prison (pronounced "Bas-tee").

When Louis XV died in 1774, he left the country on the verge of bankruptcy, and under his successor, Louis XVI, the monarchy and the country would tip over that verge and go broke. In addition to the vast expenditures the kings spent on Versailles and other residences, the wars of Louis XV in North America, the Caribbean, and Europe had severely depleted the treasury.

Louis XV's grandson, Louis XVI, did nothing to contain the spending of the court and nation. Brought up to believe that he (like his predecessors) was God's instrument on Earth, the sixteenth Louis could not see any reason why he should curtail his spending. After all, France was rich, populous, and powerful. And that was true, to a point.

As a nation, France was rich: rich in resources, rich in population, and increasingly rich in bankers. As Europe entered into trade or colonization with the rest of the world, European economies became increasingly complex. To both help handle this complexity and make a profit, the number of banks had multiplied and grown in power and influence.

Both Louis XV and Louis XVI were increasingly less effectual and interested in the running of their kingdoms. When there is a vacuum of power, people or institutions rush to fill it. In the case of Louis XV and XVI, the void left by their illustrious ancestor, Louis XIV, was filled with rich nobles and clergy, a growing middle class, and increasingly powerful banks.

In the mind of both Louises, the surest way to raise money was to increase taxes, and they did this many times. Eventually, however, a number of things can happen. First, there was simply no more money to be gathered—you can't get blood from a stone. Second, oftentimes (and especially in the case of Louis XVI), the reason there was no more money was because, despite being an increasingly modern economy, France was still dependent on agriculture, as were its nobles with their vast lands. When drought or other natural disasters hit, revenue went down, and hunger and frustration went up. Third, for a fee, the king essentially licensed out the right to tax in many areas. For instance, if a farmer was carrying his crops to market, he might have to pay a toll to cross a bridge. Farther on, if he entered the territory of another noble, he might have to pay yet another tax. This could go on ad nauseam. Theoretically, the king was supposed to receive a cut of these taxes, but they often were under-reported. Louis XIV had his own collectors, and they were closely monitored, but this was not so for his descendants. Revenues declined, fees went up, and then taxes went up, which cut into both money for investment and survival. Fourthly, the people, who were hungry, angry, and fed up with paying taxes in a country in which they had virtually no rights, might just stop paying. They might, for example, start a revolution.

In the United States, the first revolutionary slogan of 1776 was "No taxation without representation!" Since they were not represented in the English Parliament, which levied taxes on them, the American colonists insisted they either be listened to or they would start a rebellion. The American Revolution did not go unnoticed in France; it arrived in the form of soldiers returning home and in the now hundreds of newspapers and pamphlets sprouting up all over Paris. In one of the most ironic twists of fate in modern history, the French monarchy of Louis XVI funded, supported, and helped equip the Americans in their revolution. Louis did not do this out of any affinity for the Americans or their ideas. Rather, he supported the Americans to spite the English.

France and England had been either at war or in a tense peace for decades in the 18th century. In the Seven Years' War, known in the American theater as the French and Indian War, the French had suffered a humiliating defeat at the hands of the English and lost their richest colony in the New World, Quebec, along with other territories in the Caribbean and Asia.

Seeing an opportunity for revenge, Louis XVI decided to aid the Americans, especially after the colonists' victory at Saratoga in 1777. Without French aid in the American Revolution, especially at the Battle of Yorktown in 1781, the Americans would have likely lost the war.

Louis XVI got his chance to humiliate England, but he also bankrupted France to do it. Even worse, many of the officers and men in the French Army and Navy were exposed to revolutionary ideas of the Americans, with the most important ones being political freedom and the lack of a king. In the 1780s, a combination of misrule, centuries of oppression, and bad luck combined to turn France into a revolutionary tinderbox.

Lurking behind all of the issues were two inescapable facts. One was that growing seasons had been bad in France for a number of years, creating a food shortage and hunger in many parts of the country, including Paris. Hand in hand with that, the decreasing food supply, plus the taxes levied on it, forced merchants to raise prices, causing inflation to slowly get out of control.

Just after the New Year, 1789, Louis XVI made a fateful decision. He called a meeting of the Estates General, which had not been done in 175 years. The Estates General was an assembly of the three groups comprising the population of France: the nobility, the clergy, and everyone else. Actually, the "everyone else" mostly meant people of note, such as middle-class lawyers or merchants, though there were a number of poorer farmers sent to the meeting by their neighbors.

Louis XVI's primary reason for calling the meeting was to get the people's permission to raise funds—in other words, to get permission to raise taxes yet again, for both he and France were broke and living on borrowed money and financed debt. Actually, the situation for Louis had gotten so bad (not so bad that he didn't enjoy Versailles) that most of his creditors, both foreign and domestic, would not issue him any more loans. Louis also realized that there were serious issues in the country that needed addressing, with the primary ones being an unfair and arbitrary tax system and the lack of political and religious freedoms.

Politically, the big issues were the lack of freedom of speech and the issue of the *Lettres de cachet*, which were warrants of arrest without any charges. These might be levied by the king or by the king's men at court, who frequently whispered the names of their enemies in the king's ear. A person could be arrested for any number of things up to and including personal enmity.

In Paris especially, but in other cities as well, writers, artists, and newspaper publishers were all subject to strict censorship. Sometimes, these people received a warning. Sometimes, they were arrested, then presented with a *lettre de cachet* ("letters of the sign," with "the sign" meaning a royal seal).

In matters of religion, Protestantism was still officially banned, and Jews were discriminated against and made, in many cases, to pay unfair taxes. The Catholic Church owned much of the land and paid no taxes. As happened during the Reformation in other places in Europe, Frenchmen saw bishops and priests, especially in the cities, walk about in ermine robes and jewels, all the while having sworn themselves to poverty. The one exception was many times the village priest, who sometimes needed to literally beg his congregants, who were also poor, for money.

The excellent chart below shows you the main grievances of each of the three estates. This chart is broken up into nobility/clergy, the towns (meaning the middle classes), and rural parishes (meaning poor farmers and parish priests). In some cases, such as taxation, the issues overlapped. In others, they were unique to each social class.

Nobility	Towns	Rural Parishes
1. Regular Meetings of the Estates-General	1. **Taxation in general**	1. **Taxation in general**
2. **Taxation in general**	2. Provincial Estates	2. Salt tax (*gabelle*)
3. Veto on taxation for the Estates-General	3. Regular Meetings of the Estates-General	3. Tax on alcoholic beverages
4. Provincial Estates	4. Vote by head at the Estates-General	4. Salt monopoly
5. Censorship	5. Veto on taxation for the Estates-General	5. Tax on legal acts
6. Personal liberties	6. Customs duties	6. Compulsory labor services on roads
7. Allocation of taxes	7. Tax on legal acts	7. Provincial Estates
8. Government pensions	8. Censorship	8. Direct taxes (*taille*)
9. Authorizations for arrest	9. Government pensions	9. Praise of Louis XVI
10. Customs duties	10. Lack of career opportunities in the military	10. Tax exemptions and privileges enjoyed by the clergy

Illustration 22: Chart courtesy of uoregon.edu.

In January 1789, the call went out across France for the people of each estate to put forward delegates to the Estates General. It took until the beginning of May for the delegates to be chosen and make their way to Paris. When gathered, the members of the estates, with the Third Estate making up the greatest number, were hosted for a processional at Versailles, where the meeting would take place.

The members of the Third Estate wore black and gold overcoats, some of them supplied by the king for want of funds. The assembled 1,200 members waited on the grounds while Louis XVI and his wife, the unpopular Marie Antoinette, paraded before them, bejeweled and decked in regal attire. Louis was applauded. Marie Antoinette was not.

Firstly, despite her French-sounding name, Marie Antoinette was Austrian. She was of the royal Habsburg family, and her birth name was "Maria Antonia. The fact that she was a foreigner was held against her from the start. And the fact that Austria had led France into the Seven Years' War was also held against her. When she married fifteen-year-old Louis XVI in 1770, she was fourteen years old. Louis and Marie Antoinette were distant from each other for years. He was shy and suspicious of his foreign queen, and she felt rejected by him for that and by the fact that they did not have sex for seven years after their nuptials. Many in France questioned Louis's "manhood," and others questioned both of the royals' ability to have children. It is believed this problem ended in 1777 after an operation to remedy a painful condition of the king, although that's just one theory. The other is the queen lacked a sexual appetite and that the king was unable to have children. Regardless, both problems were eventually overcome. They had four children and, in time, husband and wife became devoted to each other.

Marie Antoinette was also disliked for her supposed greed, which was exacerbated by the Affair of the Diamond Necklace. Put simply, the queen was accused of trying to defraud a number of jewelers who had made a necklace for one of Louis XV's mistresses. The necklace was unbelievably lavish, and it was also unpaid for. However, though she admired the necklace, the queen did not order or want it. Someone had forged her signature, and she refused to pay for the end result. The jewelers possessed certain letters of the queen, which they then made public, and the whole of France read of the queen's duplicitous nature, but they weren't true; they had all been signed by a woman named Jeanne de la Motte. The whole affair was a scam, and most of those involved were arrested. Despite this, Marie Antoinette had already established a reputation for extravagance, which was, for the most part, true, and the affair, which took place between 1784 and 1785, further damaged both the monarchy's and the queen's reputation. (As a side note, Marie Antoinette never said, "Let them eat cake." The quote originated with Rousseau about Maria Theresa, Louis XIV's wife, and the quote had nothing to do with cake. When it was published, Marie Antoinette was ten. In actuality, Marie Antoinette, who did indeed love riches, also gave handsomely to the poor, which is much overlooked in history.)

At the Estates General, Louis, like his forebears, expected the members of the various estates to essentially approve his suggestions, many of them having been provided by his popular economics minister, Jacques Necker. However, by the spring of 1789, France was in such dire trouble that things went wrong for Louis from the start.

To begin with, the king was presented with the Cahiers de doléances—a list of complaints—which are summarized in the chart above. This was unusual, especially in regards to the first two estates, the clergy and the nobility. The length of the complaints and the overlapping nature of many of them were also a surprise, although it should be noted that the nobles and clergy had an entirely different view of them, for the most part, when compared to the Third Estate. When it came to voting on the issues, each estate got one vote. So, even though the members representing the Third Estate far outnumbered the others, they only had one vote. And they knew that the nobles and clergy were certain to vote together against the interests of the commoners on almost every issue. After a little less than a month and a half of meetings, arguments, adjournments, and anger, the members of the Third Estate did something extremely radical—they left the hall where the estates met and journeyed to a nearby tennis court (at the time, tennis was more like squash and took place indoors). There, they were joined by a small number of more progressive-minded nobles and clergymen, and they took the famous Tennis Court Oath, swearing not to adjourn until they had written a new constitution for France. They now called themselves the National Assembly.

To France, this meeting is what the meeting of the First Continental Congress is to the United States. The members of the Third Estate were breaking with centuries of history and declaring that it was they who had the power in France, not the nobles or the clergy.

Illustration 23: Drawing of the Tennis Court Oath, c. 1790 by Jacques-Louis David, who first became the propagandist for the French Revolution, then Bonaparte. In the center, a member of each estate (with the Third Estate in the middle) leads the oath.

The formation of the National Assembly, the Tennis Court Oath, and the writing of a new constitution were not seen by most of the members as an attack on the monarchy. Rather, the king was still revered by many, as they believed he was being manipulated by powerful nobles and clergy. Once he became "educated," many of the Third Estate believed that the beloved king would see that a constitutional monarchy, such as they had in England, was best for the country.

At first, Louis saw which way the wind was blowing and instructed his supporters to join with the Third Estate, agreeing to change the way votes were taken and giving each representative a vote. Soon, however, whispers in the king's ear by his court councilors, perhaps the queen and other powerful nobles and clergy, made him grow suspicious. On July 11th, 1789, Louis fired his economics minister, Necker, who had for some time encouraged the king to stop spending lavishly and to rewrite and strengthen the tax code, things that were supported by many of the Third Estate. With the firing of Necker and rumors circulating of a violent breakup of the National Assembly by the king's troops, events began to spin out of control.

On July 14th, 1789, a large mob formed in Paris, and it was joined by disenchanted members of the army. The crowd marched to the Bastille, the royal prison, where the kings of France had sent their opponents, real and imagined, to languish, be tortured, or wait for execution. Rumor had it that the prison was filled to the rafters with the king's enemies (it wasn't), and the crowd, disenchanted with the slow-moving events in and near Versailles (some fourteen miles outside Paris), were screaming for blood. The powerful symbol of the king's repression, which lay within Paris itself and consisted of thick walls with eight thirty-meter-high towers, was finally broken into by the mob. The people killed a number of soldiers and decapitated the governor (warden) and paraded his head through the streets on a pike.

July 14th (Bastille Day) is a French national holiday today, and with the Storming of the Bastille, the French Revolution began to take on a bloody life of its own.

The Storming of the Bastille sent a message not only to the king but also to the members of the National Assembly. The message to the king was clear. The message to the National Assembly was "hurry up."

Louis XVI debated sending troops into Paris, as well as other cities, to quell the violence. Then he turned about and decided to let things play out. He debated this again and again. Indecision was one of Louis's greatest faults. However, by this time, events had already spiraled out of Louis's control, although he didn't know it.

A few days after the Storming of the Bastille, the National Assembly voted for the abolition of the traditional feudal rights of the clergy and nobility. Among other things, this included freedom from many taxes and the right to demand free labor from those living on their land.

On August 26th, 1789, the National Assembly issued the Declaration of the Rights of Man and of the Citizen, which formed the underpinning of the French republics that followed, including the one that is in existence today. The Declaration of the Rights of Man was the embodiment of the ideals of the Enlightenment and the ideas of men such as Rousseau, Voltaire, and Montesquieu. The first article reads, "Men are born free and remain free and equal in rights." The second states, "The goal of any political association is the conservation of the natural and imprescriptible rights of man. These rights are liberty, property, safety and resistance against oppression." The third goes, "The principle of any sovereignty resides essentially in the Nation. No body, no individual may exercise any authority which does not proceed directly from the nation." The remaining fourteen articles include the right of free speech, freedom from arbitrary arrest, giving the power to tax to the people through their representatives, and much else. Essentially, the Declaration of the Rights of Man completely did away with the old system of nobility and privilege based on birth. However, the people still had to organize a government around the declaration and figure out what to do with the king.

Between August and October, rumors swirled throughout France. People spoke about Louis XVI ordering his troops to arrest the leaders of the National Assembly or cracking down on dissent. Some spoke of him even asking foreign powers for assistance in doing so. (It should be noted that there was some truth to these rumors.) These rumors, combined with the already angry mood in the country, the growing hunger, and rising inflation, led to another famous episode in the French Revolution: the Women's March on Versailles, sometimes known as the Wives' March.

Between October 5th and October 6th, 1789, hundreds of women from Paris marched in the rain to the Palace of Versailles. By this point, many of the women had not only become angry about the price and scarcity of food, but they had also been involved in revolutionary politics. When they arrived at the palace, they were somewhat overawed but managed to present their demands to the king. The next morning, after a tense evening, more radical voices took over, and it was determined that they should bring the king and his family to Paris, where someone could keep an eye on them. To do this, they pushed into the palace, killed a number of guards, and threatened even more radical violence, including threatening cannibalism as revenge for the food shortage in France.

The queen, her children, and servants fled in terror through a secret passage, and a number of guards were decapitated. On the grounds, troops of the National Guard, under the command of the famous Marquis de Lafayette, who aided in the American Revolution, began to talk with the remaining members of the Royal Guard, and a truce was established. Louis reluctantly agreed to accompany the women to Paris to take up residence in the Tuileries Palace.

Throughout 1790, the National Assembly passed a variety of radical laws. They abolished the nobility and created the Civil Constitution of the Clergy, which essentially stripped all clergymen of any privilege. In November, under tacit threat of force, the French clergy was instructed to take an oath to France, not the church. Most did. However, many did not, and they suffered various forms of persecution.

In June 1791, Louis and Marie Antoinette, having corresponded in secret (or so they thought) with many of the royals of Europe for aid, decided their time in France should come to an end, at least until they could marshal enough forces to regain their power and defeat the revolutionaries. On the night of June 20th, they fled in rather flimsy disguises and were discovered not far from the French border near Varennes in eastern France. They were led back to Paris, where the crowds, which had already grown hostile to the idea of any monarchy at all, essentially kept them under guard at all times.

In September 1791, a new constitution was passed with the grudging support of Louis. In sum, the Constitution of 1791 placed all the power in France in a legislative assembly. The king was basically a symbol. For the other kings, queens, and nobles of Europe, the events in France were frightening, and many European rulers had begun to hear calls for reform in their own kingdoms, and they were determined to stop them.

The meddling of Austria, the home of Marie Antoinette, in the form of plots, pronouncements, and threats was most egregious, at least in the eyes of France's new leaders. In April 1792, France declared war on Austria. In June, Prussia declared war on France. This war, which was the first of many, went back and forth, but it did cause more economic suffering in France. On August 9th, 1792, the people of Paris established their own government, known as the Commune. They decided not to take direction from the National Assembly because it was not radical enough. The next day, a mob besieged the Tuileries Palace and placed Louis XVI and Marie Antoinette under arrest, charging him with plotting with the foreign enemies of France.

Throughout the spring and summer of 1792, Louis XVI, who still had veto power over the assembly (now called the Legislative Assembly), chose to veto some of their more radical and popular proposals. Tensions within the Legislative Assembly and on the streets of Paris were exceedingly high by late August, which was when the armies of Austria and Prussia threatened mass violence against the population should any harm come to the king and his family. For many of the revolutionaries, this was the breaking point for their relationship with the monarchy. On August 10th, 1792, a large number of members from the National Guard of Paris and the militias of Marseille and Brittany marched through the capital. They attacked the Tuileries Palace, where the royal family was kept under surveillance, and slaughtered hundreds of the Swiss Guard—the king's personal guard, which he had been allowed to retain. An equal number of revolutionary soldiers and citizens were killed as well. The king, Marie Antoinette, their children, and some of their servants were arrested and taken to the Temple, a small prison in Paris.

The revolutionaries from Marseille sang a song on their march to the front, which was written by Claude Joseph Rouget de Lisle, an army captain who was, ironically, a royalist. He composed the song that became the rousing national anthem of France, "La Marseillaise," shortly after France declared war on Austria.

The Revolutionaries

At this point, it is important to identify some of the major players among the revolutionaries before we go further.

Firstly, there was the revolutionary population of Paris. Not all Parisians were revolutionaries or supported it, but by 1792, most did, and those who did not kept a very low profile. Many from the middle and upper classes who had not openly aligned themselves with the revolution early on fled Paris if they could. Many could not do so for reasons of property or business, while others believed that the worst of the revolution had passed—an error in judgment if there ever was one. Many, if not most, in the non-revolutionary middle class "dressed down" when going about in public, trying to appear as "common" as possible. If they were recognized on the street by their clothes or from their past, many were subject to harassment and violence, which only got worse as time went by.

Those doing the harassing were usually members of the working classes or those who were very poor. History has labeled these men and the women sans-culottes, or those without culottes, knee-britches, as this item of clothing was worn by the nobility and the rich. The sans-culottes wore ankle-length pants, as most people do today. Women still wore skirts or dresses, but the term "sans-culottes" is a catch-all phrase. In addition to their long pants, many of the revolutionaries wore a Phrygian cap, which was modeled after the headwear worn by ancient Roman slaves who had been given their freedom (and also many of the peoples of the Balkans and Anatolia/modern-day Turkey).

Many of the writers of the time, within France and without, referred to the sans-culottes as the "revolutionary mob," and the populations of the poorer districts of Paris (and, to a degree, other cities in France) often behaved like one. During the Reign of Terror, which began in September 1793 and continued throughout much of 1794, the sans-culottes served not only as enforcers for revolutionary leaders but also as instigators of much violence.

One of the earliest, well-known, and radical of these revolutionaries was Jean-Paul Marat (1743–1793). A relatively accomplished scientist and physician, Marat traveled Europe as a young man before settling in London for some time, becoming a relatively well-known physician. By the 1770s, he had absorbed much of the thinking of the Enlightenment and began to write tracts on despotism and the rights of man. When he returned to France in 1777, he concentrated on a scientific career and published some papers of note, especially on electricity. He also began writing about the injustices of the criminal law system in France and in much of Europe and was corresponding with Benjamin Franklin, exchanging ideas on liberty. By 1789, Marat had become one of the most radical voices in France, and he had begun publishing one of the most influential revolutionary papers of the time, *L'Ami du Peuple*, or *The Friend of the People*.

By the next year, the focus of much of his work was on plots (both real and imagined) of nobles who had fled France and were working with foreign monarchs to restore the absolute monarchy. In 1790, his writings had become too radical even for the new National Assembly, which sentenced him to a month in prison for inciting violence, but he escaped and went into hiding. By the time he came back out into public, the mood of the country had changed, as it had become more radical than before. Marat was elected to the National Convention, a branch of the Legislative Assembly.

Though he had originally opposed going to war with Austria, he soon supported it and called for a dictatorial committee of revolutionaries to govern France. In the National Convention, Marat was part of a faction called the Mountain, or the Montagnards, named for the place they occupied in the chamber. The Mountain was the more radical subset of the Jacobins, whose name stemmed from the monastery near their headquarters. The Jacobins were radicals, and they sat on the left. Opposed to them were a mixed group of moderates, led by the Girondins, many of whose early members came from the part of France known as the Gironde, and they sat on the right. Ever since that time, the terms "left" and "right" have been associated with liberals/radicals and conservatives/reactionaries, respectfully.

Marat was seen as a loose cannon, so he was kept out of most of the Montagnards' deliberations, but he was used to incite action and distrust against the movement's enemies. In April 1793, Marat was brought up on charges that he had encouraged the murder of political enemies, but he was acquitted. This move spelled the end of the Girondins, which was a more moderate voice in France, and the ascension of the Jacobins and Montagnards.

A month and a half later, in July 1793, Marat was in his bath (which he often was, as he was the victim of a painful skin disease, most likely scrofula) when a visitor called. Her name was Charlotte Corday, and she claimed to have evidence of the activities of Girondins, who had fled the capital after their downfall. Marat interviewed her in his bath and reportedly told her he would see to it that these Girondins and their sympathizers were killed. At hearing that, Charlotte Corday, who was really a Girondist sympathizer whose family had fled France in fear in 1789, stabbed Marat in the chest, killing him almost instantly. The French Revolution had its first real martyr. Corday was beheaded, and the event played a large part in ushering in the infamous Reign of Terror.

Illustration 24: The Death of Marat *by Jacques-Louis David. This romanticized portrayal became one of the most popular revolutionary images, and it was copied in print, canvas, and marble throughout France.*

Danton and Robespierre

On September 20th, 1792, the French defeated the Prussians at Valmy, which seemed to prove the value of the French Revolution and its army. On September 21st, France was proclaimed a republic, and the monarchy was abolished. The king was no longer known as King Louis XVI but rather as Citizen Louis Capet, which the revolutionaries believed was his royal house (he was actually from the House of Bourbon).

With the enemy pushed back, fever for the French Revolution high, and the king's popularity at an all-time low, the revolutionary leadership put Louis XVI on trial. Louis's trial split the revolutionaries in two. The Girondins were for keeping Louis under arrest and as a hostage, which would keep both foreign kings and French nobles who had fled France (known as the *Émigrés*, or "emigrants," though they were more like escapees) in line. The Jacobins, especially the more radical Mountain, pushed for Louis's execution.

There were many impressive personalities among the revolutionaries, but two, in particular, stand out: Georges Danton and Maximilien Robespierre.

Danton was the son of a farmer, and he had an unfortunate early childhood. As an infant, he had been attacked by a bull and run over by a herd of pigs. Making matters (and his looks) worse, Danton also survived a bout of smallpox, a regular and many times deadly scourge in virtually all parts of the world until the widespread development and adoption of vaccination techniques in the late 18th and early 19th centuries. As a result, Danton's face was uneven and disfigured by the pockmarks, which were seen on many faces during that time. Nevertheless, Danton had a reputation as being somewhat of a ladies' man when he grew older (he was widowed twice and married thrice). Danton was a tall, broad man with a deep, booming voice.

As a young man of humble background, the seminary was virtually the only place he could receive an education, and he entered one at the age of thirteen, leaving a few years later to become a clerk in Paris, where he served as a minor functionary in the *Conseil du Roi* ("Council of the King"), which was the office that governed administration throughout France.

In his years on the council and living in Paris, Danton became intimately familiar with the injustice and corruption in the government and with the disenchantment of the people around him in Paris's poorer districts. On July 14th, 1789, Danton took part in the Storming of the Bastille and confronted the troops of the famed Marquis de Lafayette. A few months later, he was elected as the representative of his Paris neighborhood and as a representative to the Paris Commune.

Danton was reportedly an incredibly fiery and charismatic figure and speaker, and his appetite for food, wine, and coarse words made him popular among the people. He also gathered about him other influential revolutionaries, such as Marat and revolutionary publisher Camille Desmoulins (a man—Camille (pronounced "Cam-ee") serves as both a male and female first name in France).

Danton soon grew to be a power to be reckoned with, protecting the less powerful and becoming the president of a political club known as the Cordeliers, formally known as the Society of the Friends of the Rights of Man and of the Citizen. He was also one of the prominent members of the Jacobins.

In the summer of 1791, Danton had to flee Paris in the aftermath of a massacre of revolutionaries, which had followed a riot near the center of the city over the future of Louis XVI after his attempted escape. Many prominent revolutionaries went into hiding for some time. Danton went to London for a few weeks.

Danton returned shortly before another revolutionary mob stormed the Tuileries Palace and put the royal family under arrest in 1792. That day, he was made the minister of justice in the Paris Commune. Danton and his associates often get overlooked in the use of terror during the revolution (Robespierre has the more infamous name in that regard), but over the next few weeks, somewhere in the neighborhood of 1,000 people were arrested without warrants and some without cause in the hunt for counter-revolutionaries. That September, Danton's Ministry of Justice, the revolutionary mood in Paris, and rumors of plots against the revolution caused an outburst of violence known as the September massacres, in which nearly 2,000 people were killed. Danton bears some of the responsibility, for he declared in a speech that anyone who was not in service of the revolution or aided it should be considered an enemy, calling for their death.

During his time as a prominent man, Danton apparently became quite wealthy. Some believed he illegally profited off the dissolution of the French East India Company, procured favorable loans for friends, and bought/sold land near his birthplace in Champagne at an exorbitant discount or profit. He also suffered the loss of two wives and children in childbirth during this period.

In March 1793, Danton and others pushed for the creation of the Revolutionary Tribunal, a special court that would deal with "enemies of the people." In April, the soon-to-be-infamous Committee of Public Safety was formed, with Danton as one of the members, though he often missed meetings, preferring to "act as a spur to action." These frequent absences may have contributed to him not being elected as a member in the July elections. A few days later, Maximilien Robespierre was elected to the Committee of Public Safety, and Danton's power slowly began to decline, though it was not obvious at the time.

In late winter/early spring of 1793, a revolt against the revolution occurred in the Vendée region of western France. The revolt was made up of royalist nobles, devout Catholics who saw the French Revolution as an attack on their faith, and many poor farmers (France, as a whole, had suffered yet another poor crop system and further inflation). Also contributing to the revolt was an order from the revolutionary government for a military draft (*levée' en masse*), which had never been done before. The Vendée revolt lasted for some months before being brutally put down. At this time, the Vendée, another rebellion in Brittany, and the population's unrest resulted in both violence and the expansion of the revolutionary government's power. The Committee of Public Safety and the Revolutionary Tribunal were both reactions to open revolt and the less violent but growing grumblings in the country.

During the summer of 1793, a power struggle between the Girondins and the Jacobins came to a head. The main issue was the arrest of Marat by the Girondins and his acquittal by the Revolutionary Tribunal. Marat was protected by both Danton and the sans-culottes, and the loss of the case put the Girondins on the defensive. The final straw was the murder of Marat by Charlotte Corday in July 1793. It was at this point that the Reign of Terror began.

During the late summer and fall of 1793, the Committee of Public Safety declared terror to be "the order of the day"—literally. Throughout France, both real and imagined "enemies of the Revolution" or "enemies of the people" were arrested and many times executed. In the winter of 1793, the "Revolutionary Razor," the guillotine, was invented by Dr. Joseph-Ignace Guillotin as a "humane" method of execution.

During the winter, Danton was at the center of events in Paris. He began calling for a slowdown of the Terror, and he also had to deal with the aforementioned accusations of financial impropriety. By February, Danton was the target of many of the more radical members of the Jacobins, and he was growing frustrated with Robespierre, who had climbed to the top position of power within the Committee of Public Safety.

During February, Danton, Robespierre, and their supporters jockeyed for the top position within Paris and France. Since Danton no longer had a seat on the Committee of Public Safety, he was in a weaker position, and his growing calls for moderation put him in Robespierre's sights. Robespierre will be discussed in a moment, but for now, suffice it to say that while he and Danton were friendly, they were never close. They were complete opposites: Danton was coarse, while Robespierre was fastidious and prim.

Convinced by his henchmen that Danton was both corrupt and working to take power for himself and his more "moderate" friends, Robespierre ordered Danton's arrest. The trial of Danton (along with many of his friends, most notably the publisher Camille Desmoulins) was a farce, devolving from charges of financial impropriety to anti-revolutionary activity and even Danton's love of food and wine as a sign of his lack of "revolutionary fervor and solidarity." Danton was not allowed to speak in his defense, though he managed to make his voice heard. However, laws preventing him from being heard and other points of procedure were rushed through the assembly to make the outcome certain. Even those who had most vocally and openly supported Danton in the past were silenced, afraid for their lives. Before he was beheaded with a group of fourteen others on April 5th, 1794, Danton predicted that "Robespierre will follow me; he is dragged down by me."

Illustration 25: A contemporary engraving of Danton's final moments.

Maximilien Robespierre did follow Danton to the guillotine, as the execution of Danton caused people to wonder if the revolution had gone too far. They started to believe that Robespierre, in particular, and his followers were beginning to act like dictators. And though he would likely have denied it, Robespierre had long let power go to his head.

Robespierre's nickname was "the Incorruptible," and honestly, if a nickname ever fit, this one did. Throughout his rise and time in power, Robespierre had more than ample opportunity to enrich himself, but he never did. Up to his death, he lived in the same simple apartment that he had lived in before the revolution began, preaching the ways of what he called "revolutionary virtue" and encouraging others to do the same.

As was mentioned above, Robespierre was the exact opposite in personality from Danton. He was prim (probably because of the example he set in his everyday life, he continued to wear an upper-class wig when many others were hiding or burning theirs), fastidious, and spoke quietly. When he did speak, though, people listened. Later in his relatively short life, they listened often from fear, but there was no doubt that Robespierre was a brilliant and well-spoken man.

Illustration 26: Coins from Year II (L'An II), 1793–the second year of the French First Republic. Two slogans can be seen. On the plaque, "Men are equal before the Law." The coin with the scales of justice, the main slogan of the revolution can be seen: "Liberté, Égalité, Fraternité." On the scales of justice, a Phrygian cap can be observed (Author's collection).

Maximilien Robespierre was born in 1758 in Arras, central France. He came from a family whose occupation had been the law since at least his grandfather and likely before. Robespierre was to follow in these footsteps. His family life was disrupted when his mother died in childbirth, taking an infant girl with her. Robespierre's father was devastated by the loss, and he fled Arras and disappeared into history. Maximilien's two younger sisters were taken in by his father's sisters, and he and his brother were raised by their mother's parents. Perhaps Robespierre took refuge in books, for he was already fully literate and reading advanced works by the ages of eight and ten, respectively. Like Danton, he attended a seminary school, as it was the only choice for the very few gifted poor and the sons of the middle class. There were no public schools, which was something that Robespierre and other revolutionaries pushed for in later years. One of his fellow pupils was Camille Desmoulins, who Robespierre later had executed along with Danton.

At school, Robespierre was fascinated with the Roman Republic (not the Empire), and he studied the works of the great Roman orators Brutus the Elder, Cato, and Cicero. In combination with the study of their oratory, Robespierre also became fascinated with the idea of Roman virtues: bravery, the incorruptibility of the mind and body, piety, and the like. Like many others of his time, he also read Rousseau's *The Social Contract,* and among the many things he gleaned from Rousseau, it was the idea of the "citizen-soldier" acting on behalf of those less fortunate that appealed to him the most.

Robespierre, however, was not a friendly person, though he had long-time acquaintances. From an early age, he seems to have interpreted these and other readings to seem to require the "virtuous man" to stand aloof above the crowd as an example, which he did until he took it too far. Some say part of the reason for Danton's break with Robespierre was Danton's impatience and boredom with Robespierre's constant preaching of "virtue."

Like other revolutionaries in both France and the United States, Robespierre believed in the theories espoused by many of the Enlightenment's great thinkers: direct democracy, the "will of the people," and equal rights under the law. He studied law for three years was after being admitted to the prestigious Sorbonne, also known as the University of Paris. He graduated among the top in his class, and immediately after, in 1782, he was given a position as a judge in the criminal court of his hometown of Arras. Interestingly enough, Robespierre resigned from that position over his opposition to the death penalty.

Over the next few years, Robespierre made a name for himself as an intellectual and writer, winning a number of prestigious prizes for essays written on criminal justice reform and the like. During this time, he became acquainted with some of the people who would make names for themselves during the French Revolution.

Robespierre was elected as one of the representatives to the Estates General from his region in 1789 after he had written an influential tract about governmental reform. During the Estates General, Robespierre began to gain his reputation as a speaker, despite his quiet voice. Some said it was the evident fervor with which he spoke that gained him adherents rather than his logic. Either way, he soon developed a coterie of followers and critics. His critics managed to keep him out of positions of power; at the time, everyone was afraid of one man standing out among the many revolutionaries. After all, they had weakened (and would soon kill) the king, and they did not want to replace him with a dictator.

Robespierre was, however, the presiding member of the Jacobin Club, the political group that would become progressively more radical and powerful as time went by. Though Robespierre has a bad name in history today, his work early on in the French Revolution should be recognized and applauded. As part of the group that worked on writing the new constitution of France, he championed universal suffrage and admission to public office and to the officer corps of the army for all who deserved it, regardless of birth or status. He also argued against religious and racial intolerance and the absolute veto of the king. In many ways, Robespierre was ahead of his time, even among revolutionaries. For example, laws mandating equality for women were reversed after his demise.

Like Danton, Robespierre called for the king's trial after the escape attempt to Varennes, and he was present at the massacre at the Champs de Mars, for which he had to go into hiding for a time. While in hiding, he kept the Jacobin Club alive, and when the danger had passed, he was greeted with a hero's welcome by the sans-culottes of Paris.

Between this time and the convening of the National Convention, which governed France from September 1792 to October 1795, Robespierre moved in and out of positions of power, sometimes being acclaimed as a hero and sometimes as a villain with the goal of dictatorship. The National Convention was the body that outlawed the monarchy and declared France a republic.

The Trial and Death of Louis XVI

In December 1792, after the shedding of much blood, the king was put on trial. Among the most prominent of those calling for the king's execution was Robespierre. During the trial, Robespierre and others accused the king of many crimes, including the murder of innocents, torture, the abuse of the law, conspiring with foreign governments to overthrow the revolution, and much more.

Still, at the beginning of the trial, many were hesitant to sentence Louis to death or even a long prison term. The power of the French monarchy went back centuries, and the French populace had been inculcated with the notion that the king was not only above the law but also a representative of God on Earth. However, in the decade and a half of Louis XVI's rule, things had gotten so bad in France that the ideas that had once sustained the French monarchy for centuries had begun to rapidly break down.

For the first part of the trial, Robespierre took ill, and his place was taken by who many considered his radical lap-dog, Louis Antoine Léon Saint-Just (simply known as Saint-Just to history), who became one of the most bloodthirsty men of the Reign of Terror. Robespierre, Saint-Just, and others argued that the king had not only conspired against the inherent rights of the people but had also plotted with foreign kings and agents, which he had. Louis was confronted with over 700 letters signed by him that asked foreign powers for aid; these had been intercepted by the revolutionaries.

The king somewhat clumsily denied the letters were his, but everyone, including himself, knew this was a lie.

The king's vain arguments and a powerful speech by a recovered Robespierre on December 3rd, 1792, convinced many that the king was a danger to the revolution and its ideals if left alive. By January 1793, the trial came to an end, with the National Convention declaring the king guilty of conspiracy and endangering the public safety and good. By mid-January, the National Convention was debating the sentence, with many Girondins and other moderates arguing for clemency and a long prison sentence. Robespierre, who was by now the acknowledged leader of the radicals of Paris and France, and the Jacobins argued for the death sentence. By a close majority, those calling for immediate execution won the day. Three days later, on January 21st, 1793, Citizen Louis Capet, formerly Louis XVI of France, was led to the guillotine and killed. His wife, Marie Antoinette, would be put on trial and executed in the same manner that October. Only their daughter, Marie-Thérèse Charlotte, would live into adulthood, as the others succumbed to illness before and shortly after the French Revolution.

Illustration 27: Famous and widely published engraving of Louis XVI's head being shown to the crowd on January 21st, 1793.

Even before the king's execution, the revolutionaries had begun to change France and its culture. They had already abolished the monarchy and nobility, and they had also weakened the clergy's power through the Civil Constitution of the Clergy, which forced the Catholic Church in France to give up much of its land, privileges, and wealth. It also forced priests and other clergymen to swear obedience to the constitution over the church. Most did so, and those who did not were often punished or sent to out-of-the-way parishes. Churchgoers who attended services by these refractory clergy were often persecuted.

The revolutionaries had declared equal rights for Protestants and Jews (at the time, there were virtually no Muslims in France), but as the French Revolution entered a new era under the influence of Robespierre, the whole idea of a Judeo-Christian deity came under attack.

When Robespierre entered the Sorbonne and began his rise to notability through his writings, he was an advocate of religious tolerance, like many of the later revolutionaries and much of the educated populace of France, especially in Paris. This continued when the revolution first began in 1789. However, as time went by and he saw how entrenched the ideas of the Catholic Church were in France, both in regard to spiritual matters and earthly ones, that position began to change.

Among the many things the Protestant Reformation had changed in much of Europe, including pockets of France, was to make the Bible available in local languages, not just Latin, as it had been for centuries. With this move, literate people began to read the Bible for themselves and develop ideas that were different than those held by the church. Many of those who could not read were read to or instructed in the Bible by men and women who had read the text themselves. Sometimes, they came up with radically different conclusions than those held by the pope and the Catholic hierarchy.

In those parts of Europe that had turned to Protestantism, such as England, much of northern Germany, Scandinavia, the Netherlands, and much of Switzerland, new ideas about Christ and Christian doctrine arose. During the period of tolerance between Henry IV's rule Louis XIV's revocation of religious rights, a sizable Protestant minority had grown in France, but it was forced underground under Louis XIV. In the time leading up to the French Revolution, some Protestants felt a bit more freedom to practice their religious convictions, but there was hardly religious freedom as we know it in the West today.

In 1793, as the Reign of Terror began, the radicals among the Jacobins and others promoted the Cult of Reason, and it was actually supported by the state as an "atheistic religion" devoted to the idea that human reason and scientific knowledge could solve most or all of the world's mysteries and/or problems. Among historians, the Age of Enlightenment was preceded by the Age of Reason, which was made famous by the works of Isaac Newton, René Descartes, Francis Bacon, Gottfried Leibniz, and many others. Thus, "reason" gave way to "enlightenment," and for the revolutionaries in Paris, Christianity (in particular, Catholic Christianity) was a superstitious cult created by the few for their enrichment and the oppression of the masses. Many Protestant sects, particularly the sects that had arisen in Switzerland and eastern France that incorporated the idea of predestination, were another way of elites holding the masses down. To counter the thousands of years of religious oppression in France, the Cult of Reason was formed by two prominent revolutionaries, Joseph Fouché and Antoine-François Momoro.

The Cult of Reason stressed the idea of civic duty according to the ideas of the Enlightenment philosophers, such as Voltaire and Rousseau, and refused to allow "reason" as an idea to be personified as a god, meaning they didn't want abstract statues or paintings of "reason" to be created for purposes of worship. The

Cult of Reason and adherence to it became a trademark of many of the revolutionaries, especially of the sans-culottes, who had become the most violent supporters of the revolution and the Reign of Terror. One of the more interesting people of the period, a Prussian who adopted French citizenship, Anacharsis Cloots (he took the French name Jean-Baptiste du Val-de-Grâce), declared that there would be only one god—the people. He was later guillotined by Robespierre.

After Robespierre rose to the top of the Committee of Public Safety, he rejected the Cult of Reason and replaced it with something he had developed himself: the Cult of the Supreme Being. This happened for many reasons. Firstly, many of the Enlightenment greats in both Europe and North America were not atheists; they were Deists, meaning they believed in a supreme being that gave rise and order to the universe and life on Earth but did not truly involve itself in the everyday lives of people and especially did not call for the giving of money to a church for the forgiveness of sins.

Robespierre was a Deist as well, as were many of his friends and other revolutionaries throughout France. He believed that the masses of people were eager to be free of the oppression of the Catholic Church but not willing to give up the idea of a god. His Cult of the Supreme Being supplanted the Cult of Reason and became the official religion of France for a very short time.

Robespierre also believed that the idea of a god was necessary for social order, as people needed to answer to a higher power or authority for human society to remain orderly. He often quoted Voltaire: "If God did not exist, it would be necessary to invent him." For Robespierre, "the Incorruptible," religion was the path to the virtues he had believed in and extolled since he was a child.

At this point in time (around the summer of 1794), Robespierre had risen to control not only Paris but also France through the Committee of Public Safety and its offices and agents throughout the country. He had begun to strike at his enemies in the fall of 1793, and this continued into the spring and summer of 1794. This was the infamous Reign of Terror, and some of its first victims were not only political foes of Robespierre and the Jacobins but also men who had pushed the Cult of Reason, such as Fouché, Momoro, and Cloots.

On the twentieth day of Prairial in the Year II (the revolutionaries created a new calendar to mark the departure from the old ways), the Festival of the Supreme Being was held in Paris, as well as smaller ones in towns throughout France. The festival was designed by Jacques-Louis David, who painted the famous *Death of Marat* and would soon immortalize Napoleon, and it was similar to a Roman-style event, with some actually wearing togas and olive wreaths. A man-made mountain was erected in the Champs-de-Mars (the "Field of Mars") in Paris, and many weren't exactly sure what to do and sort of just milled around, waiting. The worst part was a long, dry speech by Robespierre, who came down the mountain in the style of Moses. To many, the Festival of the Supreme Being was a sign that the revolution had gotten out of hand and that a small group of people, led by Robespierre, was setting themselves up as dictators.

The Revolutionary Calendar[1]

Vendémiaire Sept.–Oct.	Brumaire Oct.–Nov.	Frimaire Nov.–Dec.	Nivôse Dec.–Jan.	Pluviôse Jan.–Feb.	Ventôse Feb.–March	Germinal March–April	Floréal April–May	Prairial May–June	Messidor June–July	Thermidor July–Aug.	Fructidor Aug.–Sept.	Jours sans-culottides September
1 22	1 22	1 21	1 21	1 20	1 19	1 21	1 20	1 20	1 19	1 19	1 18	1 17
2 23	2 23	2 22	2 22	2 21	2 20	2 22	2 21	2 21	2 20	2 20	2 19	2 18
3 24	3 24	3 23	3 23	3 22	3 21	3 23	3 22	3 22	3 21	3 21	3 20	3 19
4 25	4 25	4 24	4 24	4 23	4 22	4 24	4 23	4 23	4 22	4 22	4 21	4 20
5 26	5 26	5 25	5 25	5 24	5 23	5 25	5 24	5 24	5 23	5 23	5 22	5 21
6 27	6 27	6 26	6 26	6 25	6 24	6 26	6 25	6 25	6 24	6 24	6 23	
7 28	7 28	7 27	7 27	7 26	7 25	7 27	7 26	7 26	7 25	7 25	7 24	
8 29	8 29	8 28	8 28	8 27	8 26	8 28	8 27	8 27	8 26	8 26	8 25	
9 30	9 30	9 29	9 29	9 28	9 27	9 29	9 28	9 28	9 27	9 27	9 26	
10 1	10 31	10 30	10 30	10 29	10 28	10 30	10 29	10 29	10 28	10 28	10 27	
11 2	11 1	11 1	11 31	11 30	11 1	11 31	11 30	11 30	11 29	11 29	11 28	
12 3	12 2	12 2	12 1	12 31	12 2	12 1	12 1	12 31	12 30	12 30	12 29	
13 4	13 3	13 3	13 2	13 1	13 3	13 2	13 2	13 1	13 1	13 31	13 30	
14 5	14 4	14 4	14 3	14 2	14 4	14 3	14 3	14 2	14 2	14 1	14 31	
15 6	15 5	15 5	15 4	15 3	15 5	15 4	15 4	15 3	15 3	15 2	15 1	
16 7	16 6	16 6	16 5	16 4	16 6	16 5	16 5	16 4	16 4	16 3	16 2	
17 8	17 7	17 7	17 6	17 5	17 7	17 6	17 6	17 5	17 5	17 4	17 3	
18 9	18 8	18 8	18 7	18 6	18 8	18 7	18 7	18 6	18 6	18 5	18 4	
19 10	19 9	19 9	19 8	19 7	19 9	19 8	19 8	19 7	19 7	19 6	19 5	
20 11	20 10	20 10	20 9	20 8	20 10	20 9	20 9	20 8	20 8	20 7	20 6	
21 12	21 11	21 11	21 10	21 9	21 11	21 10	21 10	21 9	21 9	21 8	21 7	
22 13	22 12	22 12	22 11	22 10	22 12	22 11	22 11	22 10	22 10	22 9	22 8	
23 14	23 13	23 13	23 12	23 11	23 13	23 12	23 12	23 11	23 11	23 10	23 9	
24 15	24 14	24 14	24 13	24 12	24 14	24 13	24 13	24 12	24 12	24 11	24 10	
25 16	25 15	25 15	25 14	25 13	25 15	25 14	25 14	25 13	25 13	25 12	25 11	
26 17	26 16	26 16	26 15	26 14	26 16	26 15	26 15	26 14	26 14	26 13	26 12	
27 18	27 17	27 17	27 16	27 15	27 17	27 16	27 16	27 15	27 15	27 14	27 13	
28 19	28 18	28 18	28 17	28 16	28 18	28 17	28 17	28 16	28 16	28 15	28 14	
29 20	29 19	29 19	29 18	29 17	29 19	29 18	29 18	29 17	29 17	29 16	29 15	
30 21	30 20	30 20	30 19	30 18	30 20	30 19	30 19	30 18	30 18	30 17	30 16	

[1] The Revolutionary (or Republican) Calendar was in official use between 22 September 1793 (1st Vendémiaire of the Year II) to the end of 1805 (11th Nivôse of the Year XIV). In leap-years (1796, 1800, 1804), 11th Ventôse corresponded to 29 February and the extra day of the Republican Year was 'found' by adding a sixth 'jour sans-culottide' (or 'jour complémentaire') to the five shown above.

Illustration 28: The French Revolutionary calendar. Names of months were taken from the natural and agricultural characteristics of the month. Hence, the last month of summer was "Fructidor" for "fruit."

By the summer of 1794, the people of France and Paris, in particular, had grown weary of the Reign of Terror. Initially, they supported the Terror as a way to either eliminate or cow the enemies of the revolution. These are the times depicted in Dickens's famous *Tale of Two Cities*, with its revolutionary crowds screaming for blood, egged on by sans-culottes and revolutionary women, such as the fictional Madame Defarge.

The Reign of Terror lasted from early September 1793 to the end of July 1794, which was when Robespierre and his supporters went to the guillotine themselves. During these ten months or so, it is estimated that some 20,000 or more people were executed by official decree. Many others were killed without record. During the Terror, revolts took place throughout France, and many of those opposing the Terror or the French Revolution were killed. It is important to note that the Terror didn't just abruptly end; it slowly petered out as people grew weary and moved on to another form of revolutionary government.

Throughout France, people turned on neighbors, rushing to report them for "anti-revolutionary activities" or as "enemies of the people." This allowed them to get revenge for old arguments, fights over property and businesses, and even love affairs. Once a person was accused, it was very hard to find innocence, especially since most cases were "tried" by People's Tribunals that met either every day, in the case of Paris and other large cities, or irregularly, in the case of smaller towns. Either way, a lack of harsh prison sentences or executions showed a "lack of revolutionary vigor" and could often get those on the tribunals in hot water themselves. As Danton had reportedly said, "The Revolution, like Saturn, devours its own children."

The total dead through officially sanctioned executions, of which many were signed off by Robespierre, may never be known. Estimates run from a low 20,000 to over 100,000 or more. What is known is that the Reign of Terror and the rule of the Committee of Public Safety was in many ways the precursor to the multitude of totalitarian governments of the 20th century.

In the end, Robespierre, who had begun as a relatively tolerant man, gradually became convinced that he could lead France into a life of incorruptible "virtue." The problem was, as he neared the end of his life, Robespierre and those around him began to see enemies everywhere. Not that he didn't have them—he just thought that there were many more than there were. Making things worse, there had been assassination attempts on Robespierre and others close to him. Robespierre pushed through laws on dissent that rankled other revolutionaries and made them think about the reasons the revolution had begun in the first place.

Robespierre and his cronies also spread lies about people who dared speak against them or the Terror. Toward the end of the Terror, the violence of the Committee of Public Safety actually increased, with the mobs of sans-culottes, who Robespierre and others secretly despised, being set upon their enemies.

By late July, many of those in power had had enough of Robespierre, Saint-Just, and the Committee of Public Safety. Robespierre had made many enemies throughout the revolutionary ranks, accusing them of leniency, corruption, and much else. Some of this was true, but much of it was false. On July 27th, 1794, the National Convention met in Paris. News came from the frontlines that the French had defeated the Austrians yet again, and many in the National Convention supported an easing of the Terror as the war wound down. Knowing that this would lead to a decrease in his power, Robespierre and his adherents protested, but many outside of his circle began to openly accuse him of wanting to be a dictator.

Robespierre and Saint-Just had made speeches in the Jacobin Club earlier in the week, accusing many in the National Convention of being traitors and working against the revolution. They planned to give the same speeches in the convention hall, but as they attempted to do so, they were shouted down every time they tried to speak. Member after member rose to speak against them, including a leading revolutionary named Jean-Lambert Tallien, the commissioner of the National Convention. Tallien's wife was an influential critic of Robespierre, as well as an early friend of Joséphine de Beauharnais, who would become the wife of Napoleon, and Robespierre had her arrested.

Robespierre's attack on the wife of the commissioner of the National Convention was the last straw. Tallien, as commissioner, made a passionate speech against Robespierre and called for a vote against him and his followers. Subsequently, Robespierre, Saint-Just, and a number of others were arrested. These men escaped to the Hôtel de Ville (city hall), where, that night, a mob besieged them and wounded Robespierre in the jaw, allowing curiosity seekers to gawk at him in agony. The next day, "the Incorruptible" and about twenty others were executed on the Place de la Concorde, the same place where Louis XVI and Danton had lost their lives.

History knows this episode as both the end of the Reign of Terror and the Thermidorian Reaction, named for the month of the French Revolutionary calendar in which it took place.

Illustration 29: The Thermidorian Reaction against Robespierre in the National Convention.

After the death of Robespierre, the Terror was halted, and the revolution headed in a slightly more conservative direction. A new form of government and yet another constitution were formed. The executive branch of this government was called the Directory, and it lasted four years, from November 1795 to November 1799. The

Directors were five men in an attempt to prevent the rise of another Robespierre, and a bicameral legislature, similar to the American system, picked the Directors.

The Directors were equipped with weak executive powers, which meant the power devolved to the two legislative houses, so not a lot got done. Corruption was rampant, though. Since the Directors did not have the "power of the purse" and the legislative branch consisted of some 600 members from two houses, with competing interests keeping things at a virtual standstill legally, many turned to bribery. Naturally, citizens who had just been through literal hell asked themselves if they had gotten rid of a corrupt monarchy for a corrupt Directory.

However, one of the lasting achievements of the Directory cannot be overstated. They established the first modern public school system, which was open to virtually everyone. Within a generation or two, France had the highest literacy rate on the planet, and in the late 1800s, it was home to some of the world's greatest scientists, especially in the fields of chemistry, medicine, and biology.

Unfortunately, this was outweighed by corruption, and though many of the actions of the Directory were attempts to cement the gains of the revolution in perpetuity, some of the rules, both said and unsaid, on wealth and personal privilege were relaxed. Many noble emigrants returned, and many sons of the upper-middle classes began to take on noble airs. In fact, in Paris and some of the largest cities, gangs of what became known as the Muscadin ("musk wearers"—expensive perfume for men) or the Gilded Youth roamed the streets looking for trouble, attacking whom they deemed as radicals and attempting to reestablish their life of privilege. For many of these Gilded Youth, these attacks were revenge for the attacks made on them or their families during the Terror.

Additionally, and we will discuss this further in the following chapter, France had been at war for a great deal of the revolutionary period and had made enemies across Europe and the English Channel. This had happened not only because of the losses accrued on the battlefield but also because French revolutionary ideas had begun to spring up within many European territories. Monarchs, nobles, and the burgeoning middle classes in these countries believed their positions and possibly their heads were threatened by revolutionaries motivated by the events in France. There was even trouble in the United States, where the French ambassador threatened George Washington with mob violence in an attempt to strongarm the American president in supporting French ambitions in the New World and against England.

So, as the 19th century approached, France was still in a period of tremendous change, and its people were beginning to tire of it. After a decade of revolution, terror, wars both domestic and foreign, and great change, many of the people in France wanted a period of peace and stability.

The French Revolution was so radical, so involved, and so politically intricate that it is hard to cover them all in an introductory history such as this. At the end of this book, you will find a number of excellent titles that will both broaden and deepen your knowledge of this earth-shaking event—and it was earth-shaking, for nothing in Europe would ever be the same afterward.

Before we move forward into the next chapter, it is important to examine the lasting effects of the French Revolution.

Perhaps first and foremost, it ended feudalism in France and, for a time, the idea of hereditary privilege. No longer were nobles and the clergy, which accounted for about 3 percent of the population, the holders of almost 97 percent of the land and most of the country's wealth. Though the French monarchy would return after the fall of Napoleon, the idea of advancement through merit rather than birth became more established in France and later in most of western Europe.

The French Revolution also removed the Catholic Church from its place of dominance in French society. Though a civil war of sorts would continue to simmer between devout Catholics and secularists in France into the 20th century, the revolution removed Catholicism from its position of power and influence in much of French life. It also moved religious toleration forward—no longer, at least on paper, were Protestants and Jews discriminated against. Though France would be shaken by a major scandal in the late 19th century regarding religious and ethnic discrimination, the revolutionaries took the first steps toward broad religious toleration in Europe.

As was previously mentioned, a system of public schools was established, leading France to become one of the most educated nations on the planet. Although the words "nation" and "country" have been used throughout this book to describe France and other territories, it was not until the French Revolution that France and many of the areas of Europe affected by the French Revolution were identified as a "nation" and not a "kingdom." Now, France would be recognized as not only an area of land but also a region of ideals, a specific culture, and equality under the law.

In the United States during the 1780s and most of the 1790s, the idea of political parties and specific ideologies were relatively unknown. It was in revolutionary France that political ideology (the notion that a set or competing sets of political ideals should shape society) was born. The ideas of a liberal "Left," a conservative "Right," and "moderates" were developed in France in the 1790s.

Though many of the French revolutionaries were inspired by the events of the American Revolution, the Americans did not specifically set out to spread their political ideals to other nations in order to "liberate" them from monarchies or other elites. The French revolutionaries most certainly did. The French Revolution ushered in what historians call the Age of Revolution, which swept

Europe, as well as South and Central America, for most of the 19th century.

In combination with the above, the French Revolution, though it had its tyrannical Reign of Terror, helped spread democratic and liberal ideals throughout Europe and the world. Today, in the United States, in particular, the word "liberal" has taken on a different meaning in some quarters, but historically, the words "liberal" or "liberalism" meant the spread of ideas, such as equality under the law, mass education, and the freedom of speech, religious tolerance, and much more. Though the French Revolution reached its extremes, today's democratic societies around the world owe the French revolutionaries a huge debt.

Lastly, the impact of the changes wrought by the revolution was such that historians use the period as the dividing line for a new era: the modern era.

Illustration 30: Though the painting Liberty Leading the People *was created in 1830 by Eugène Delacroix to commemorate another revolution in France in that year, the image perfectly captures both the ideals and events of the earlier 1789 French Revolution.*

Chapter 9 – Vive l'Empereur!

One of the many things that students in introductory history classes are always astounded by is how the French Revolution, with its rejection of Louis XVI, morphed into an even grander form of monarchy at the start of the 19th century under Napoleon Bonaparte.

In actuality, the evolution from the radical French Revolution to Napoleon's government is not all that surprising, at least to us today. To the men and women of France and Europe at the time, it certainly was. The cycle of the French Revolution, from localized revolts to violent unplanned uprisings to organized revolution and so on, is familiar to us now and has played itself out many times since 1789, albeit in slightly different forms. In most cases, whether it's an emperor or some other stabilizing force, the revolution is scaled back, though not to the point where its necessary changes are done away with. Since the French Revolution was the first truly modern revolution, this cycle was unfamiliar at the time (the American version began with a revolt against a "foreign" king and then developed or solidified its revolutionary ideas after the conflict was over).

Napoleon declared himself the emperor of the French in 1804. He had ruled the country as the first consul since 1799/1800, and he was the leader of the state in all but name by the time he took his imperial title. During the run-up to his coronation, from 1799 to 1804, there were some royalists (supporters of the Bourbon family, of which Louis XVI was a part) that thought Napoleon would use his power (meaning the army) to install and protect Louis XVIII (Louis XVI's brother) after restoring some sort of order to France.

Napoleon told the would-be king's representatives in no uncertain terms that the only way that the Bourbons would regain the throne was "over 100,000 corpses." And that went for the rest of the nobility's and clergy's feudal rights and former lands. No, Napoleon would be an emperor, but he would be a revolutionary one, and when he could not be that, he would make his own rules. This was even more astounding, for in the eyes of many Frenchmen, Napoleon Bonaparte was a foreigner. He came from the newly acquired Italian-speaking island of Corsica, which was the former possession of the Republic of Genoa.

Corsica

Napoleon was born in Ajaccio, Corsica's capital city, in 1769. That year was an auspicious one in many ways, at least for France, Napoleon, and Corsica. Corsica is a large island that lies about halfway between southern France and northern Italy in the Mediterranean Sea. From 1559 to 1755, the island had been a possession of the Republic of Genoa, a province in northern Italy. In 1729, the Corsicans began a decades-long struggle for independence, which was led by Pasquale Paoli and his family. By 1755, the Corsicans had established control over most of the island with the exception of two Genoese fortresses, and they established a republic with a constitution written for them by Enlightenment philosophe Jean-Jacques Rousseau.

Unfortunately for the Corsicans, their republic was not recognized by any significant power in Europe, and in 1769, the King Louis XV of France purchased Corsica from a cash-strapped Genoa.

Illustration 31: Corsica, with capital Ajaccio marked "A." (Courtesy Google Maps)

The Bonaparte family (the name was actually spelled "Buonaparte") had emigrated to Corsica in the 1500s from Tuscany, the region that includes Genoa. Initially, the Buonapartes and other immigrants from the mainland were looked upon as foreigners and strangers by the native Corsicans, who had their own language and culture. However, over the centuries, families like the Buonapartes integrated into Corsican culture, and by the late 18th century, they had no real roots in mainland Europe. Still, for many years, Napoleon considered himself Tuscan or Italian rather than Corsican. (One must remember that Italy did not become a united nation until the late 1860s, though).

Napoleon's parents, Carlo and Letizia, had two children die in infancy before having Joseph, Napoleon, Lucien, Elisa, Louis, Pauline, Caroline, and Jerome. Later in his career, Napoleon placed his brothers on the thrones of various European countries, but they were all relative failures. For instance, his brother Joseph fled Spain after his unpopular term as king, settling in the United States, with a home in Bordentown, New Jersey, near the site of Washington's crossing of the Delaware.

The Buonapartes were descended from minor Tuscan nobility, and like many immigrant families on Corsica, they lived as such. They took on upper-class styles (wigs, culottes for men, stockings, etc.) and considered themselves the elite of the island. Napoleon's father, Carlo, was a lawyer and diplomat, which put him near the top of Corsican society. Carlo also took part in the war of resistance against the French when they first came to the island. However, when that resistance was finally quelled, Carlo became the island's representative to the court of Louis XVI at Versailles.

Naturally, this meant that Napoleon and his siblings (especially his brothers) were afforded a privileged life and access to education, which most Corsicans did not have. It was evident to virtually everyone that Napoleon was gifted. He read books far beyond what most children his age were capable of and excelled in math. History, especially military history, was his favorite subject, and he read voraciously, especially on his hero, Alexander the Great, and the history of Rome. One of his favorite activities was to recreate famous battles with his collection of lead soldiers. Virtually everyone that came into contact with him recognized that he was on a different level from most boys his age and even many adults. Napoleon was also known for being rowdy, independent-minded, and rebellious. His mother, to whom he was devoted, kept him in line.

In January 1779, at the age of nine, Napoleon was sent to the mainland French city of Autun in northeastern France to attend a religious academy. In May of that year, he transferred to a military academy in roughly the same area.

For almost any nine-year-old boy, being over 600 miles away from home is traumatic. For Napoleon, it was hell.

It wasn't until he was ten that Napoleon began to really understand French. Prior to his going to school in France, there had been no reason to learn it. His family had spoken Italian at home, and he spoke Corsu (Corsica's native language) as well. At school, he was bullied incessantly for his bad French, as it had an Italian/Corsican accent. He was seen as a rustic farm boy even though his father had been the Corsican delegate to the court of Louis XVI. In pre-revolutionary France, virtually all of the boys and young men in attendance at schools were of noble families, and they looked down on Frenchmen without titles. It is no surprise that they would look down on a foreigner.

Illustration 32: Bonaparte the Novice *by Maurice Realier-Dumas, 1894.*

It was not only his poor (but rapidly improving) French skills that made Bonaparte stand out like a sore thumb. In a time when people were, on average, much shorter than they are today, he was on the shorter side—at about 5'4" tall. Napoleon did not help his case much either. He withdrew into himself when he could, but among others, he sometimes acted arrogantly, as if he knew more than they. Still worse, he did, and he never tired of letting anyone forget it. Because of his social exile, Bonaparte devoted himself utterly to his studies, especially math, history, and cartography.

If you had asked most of his fellow students at the military school at Brienne what Napoleon was destined for, the vast majority would have likely said that he would've been sent to a far-flung post, likely in the West Indies, where he would remain a low-level officer for the rest of his life.

However, to a few of his fellow students and quite a number of his instructors, Bonaparte stood out. His leadership and skill showed during the now-famous snowball fights, where he would rally his side to victory (often the snowballs were loaded with rocks), and to the discerning and mature eye, Napoleon was impressive in every way. He seemed to think faster than his fellows, he was more decisive, and he had an uncanny ability with artillery. From Brienne, he went to the military academy (the École Militaire) in Paris in 1784 for a two-year officer course. He graduated in one year and was sent to Valence in the south of France as a lieutenant in the artillery.

From about 1787 to about the time of the French Revolution, Napoleon became enamored with two things: republicanism, as advocated by writers such as Rousseau, and Corsican politics. It was unusual, but Napoleon somehow seemed to be able to negotiate or wrangle his way into an extraordinary amount of leave, and he spent most of the years between 1789 and 1792 in Corsica, though he did travel back and forth between France and the island often.

In the days before the revolution, Napoleon was aligned with one of his childhood heroes, Pasquale Paoli, who had fought for Corsican independence from Genoa and was now agitating for the island's independence from France. Napoleon at first supported Paoli's cause, as he still saw himself as a Corsican, not a Frenchman or an Italian. However, as the French Revolution grew nigh, Napoleon began to become more and more supportive of the republican cause and less supportive of Paoli's. While men and women in France were giving up their lives to change the system of absolute monarchy in France, Paoli seemed to be moving in the opposite direction and setting himself up as the power in Corsica. Over time, Napoleon and Paoli became estranged, which was made worse when Napoleon's father, Carlo, who had fought and supported Paoli in the war against Genoa, aligned himself against Paoli's faction in the Corsican Assembly and against Corsican independence.

Napoleon eventually became an adherent of the radical beliefs of the Jacobins in the initial days of the revolution, and he was promoted to a captain in the Republic of France's new army, despite having taken part in a riot against the French in his initial days back in Corsica. His repeated visits and extended stays on the island, sometimes without leave, did not seem to count against him either.

In 1793, Napoleon's support of the revolution led to his final split with Paoli. He supported a French attack on a smaller Corsican-held island, and both he and his family were forced to flee Corsica for France in 1793. Up to this point, Napoleon had considered himself a Corsican, not a Frenchman. Napoleon's birth name was Napoleone di Buonaparte, which was an Italian name. From the time of the split, he began calling himself Napoléon ("Nah-poh-lay-ohn") Bonaparte—the French version.

Napoleon was a relatively well-known man in Corsica, but in France, he was just another junior officer in a rapidly growing army. Historians have debated for centuries over which of Napoleon's personal characteristics was the most dominant. Some say his audacity, others his intelligence, but no matter what they believe, one of the most dominant features was his ambition. From his earliest days at school, when he realized that he was far beyond his fellow students in ability, Napoleon was ambitious. To us, that is no surprise. We know that he rose from relative obscurity to become the emperor of much of Europe. He may be the most widely written-about personality of all time today, but in the 1790s, France was full of ambitious young men. Now, because of the French Revolution and the Declaration of the Rights of Man, these young men were free to exercise their intelligence and abilities, even if they were not born nobles.

Napoleon was present when the revolutionary mob attacked the Tuileries Palace, which held the king and queen. This attack, the first real move toward putting the monarchs on trial and executing them, was a bloody affair, and Napoleon witnessed it firsthand from his apartment window. During the attack, the Royal Guard that Louis had been allowed to keep were essentially torn apart limb from limb, with some of them having their head mounted on pikes and paraded through the streets of Paris. The fury of the uncontrollable mob frightened Napoleon to his core, and he vowed to never allow such violent anarchy if he was in a position to stop it, which he later was.

In 1793, Bonaparte was stationed in the south of France, near the important port city of Toulon. Toulon itself was in the hands of royalist Frenchmen, and they had committed not only the "sin" of supporting the old regime (the Bourbon family and the nobility) but also of inviting the troops and ships of France's most hated enemy, the English, into the city.

Napoleon was given command of the artillery on the hills surrounding Toulon. The heights were a great advantage, for the British ships were not able to elevate their guns to reach Napoleon's position. For most of his career, Napoleon's men loved him. They learned that, in his eyes, they always came first. He made sure, to the best of his amazing abilities, that they were fed, clothed, and well-cared for. He also knew, especially as a younger junior officer, that if he did those things, his men would follow him almost anywhere.

The Siege of Toulon had been going on for some months when Napoleon was given charge of the French guns. He soon had new emplacements dug and secured more ammunition and weapons from nearby French posts. Within a relatively short amount of time, he had reduced the city's defenses to the point where republican troops could assault the city with some degree of surety that they would succeed. And they did succeed. On December 19th, 1793, the British and French royalists in the city surrendered. In the assault on the city, Napoleon, leading from the front, was wounded in the leg. Many of the royalist soldiers, who had either surrendered or were captured in the battle, were executed en masse by firing squad or bayonet. However, this was not at Napoleon's command. He neither had the authority to countermand this order, which came from the powerful revolutionary figure Paul Barras, nor was he even in the city, for he was elsewhere being treated for his wounds.

Not only did his role in the victory at Toulon come to the attention of the leading revolutionaries in Paris, but in his time in the south of France, Napoleon had also authored a pamphlet entitled *Le souper de Beaucaire* (*The Supper at Beaucaire*). In it, Napoleon recounted a dinner he had held for some of the leading citizens in the area in which he was stationed before the Siege of Toulon. Napoleon's goal at the dinner was to allay the fears his dinner guests had of the revolution and the changes it brought in its wake. The other purpose of the pamphlet, the more important of the two to Napoleon, was to illustrate to the powers that be, whether in the south of France or in Paris, that he was a tried and true revolutionary, an officer they could count on. He likely succeeded more in the second purpose than the first, for along with his victory, *The Supper at Beaucaire* reassured the men in Paris that they had a new bright star in the military that they could trust.

Illustration 33: Painted after Napoleon's rise, The Supper at Beaucaire, *by Jean Lecomte du Nouÿ, depicts not only the event but also adds symbolism. Napoleon (standing) tells his guests about the glories of the revolution—he is literally bringing them "into the light," as shown by the candlelight beaming in their faces.*

During the Siege of Toulon, Napoleon had risen in rank from captain to major to adjutant general (a staff officer). After his victory at Toulon, Napoleon was named brigadier general—and all this by the age of twenty-four. This was both a testament to his ability and a symbol of the new order in France, that a man could rise as high as his ability, not birth, would take him.

In Paris, Maximilien Robespierre's brother, Augustin, the government's commissioner to the army, wrote to his powerful brother at the beginning of 1794 and told him of the "transcendent merit" of the man from Corsica. In February of that year, Napoleon was given command of the artillery of the French Army of Italy. The French had been fighting there, as well as in the Rhine River area, hoping to both repel Austrian invaders and spread the ideals of the French Revolution.

Even today, any ambitious man is going to make enemies or at least arouse suspicion and jealousy. And it was no secret that Robespierre and the radicals on the Committee of Public Safety had placed Napoleon in his position. He arrived in February 1793, about halfway into the Reign of Terror. Four and a half months later, Robespierre, his brother, and many other leading figures of the Reign of Terror were beheaded. As a result, Napoleon, whom Augustin had referred to as "Robespierre on horseback," fell under suspicion and was charged with conspiracy and treason. He was put under house arrest in Nice for a time.

His connections and his lack of participation in the government or the Reign of Terror led to his release after two weeks. Napoleon took part in an abortive attempt by the French to take Corsica's southern island neighbor Sardinia from the British and the province of Savoy from their Italian allies. He was then given an infantry position in the west of France to help put down the royalist rebellion in the Vendée, but at the time, the artillery branch was the elite branch of the army. To get out of the assignment, Napoleon pulled an old children's trick: he faked an illness. He was then assigned a dreary job as a military cartographer.

Many believe these assignments came to him for two reasons. He had been close to Robespierre, and his ambition was becoming very well known. In Paris, Napoleon began to move in exclusive circles, especially among the salons of the wealthy middle class. This gave him an opportunity to meet some of the leading figures of the time, as well as their wives, whom he knew could influence their husbands. It also made himself and his ambitions known. The salons might have engaged in gossip and rumors, but they also led to important and influential connections.

During this time, he became engaged to Désirée Clary, the daughter of a rich businessman from Marseille. Napoleon's older brother Joseph was already married to Désirée's older sister, Julie. For a time, Napoleon was passionately in love with Désirée, and he even wrote a short novel, *Clisson et Eugénie*, based on their story. However, Napoleon met the widow Joséphine de Beauharnais at one of the Paris salons and fell almost instantly head over heels in love. The engagement to Désirée was off, and Napoleon and Joséphine, who was six years older than the general, which displeased his family greatly, married in 1796. Désirée went on to marry one of the men who became a marshal under Napoleon, Jean Bernadotte, who later became the king of Sweden and Norway. Désirée became a queen, and their descendants are on the throne of Sweden to this day.

It can be said with relative confidence that Napoleon and Joséphine loved each other to the end of their days, though he divorced her in 1810 for the younger, and, more importantly, more fertile and politically well-connected, Marie Louise, the princess of Austria. He had a son with her, Napoleon François Joseph Charles Bonaparte. Napoleon II was born in 1811 and given the title "King of Rome." He lived a short life—he died in 1832 of tuberculosis, which was made worse by pneumonia.

Napoleon and Joséphine are remembered for a number of reasons. First, he was madly in love with her. She seemed to love him as well but not with the same fervor. She was also six years older than him and a widow, which caused a bit of a scandal. When they divorced, Napoleon let her keep her titles, income, and home at Malmaison. Most importantly, throughout their marriage, he occasionally took her advice, which was often good. This usually came in the form of political or politically social advice: how he related to people, how he should present himself, reports of events at home while he was on campaign, etc. Much of the time, she was correct. She died suddenly while walking with the visiting Tsar Alexander I of Russia in 1814. At the time, Napoleon was in exile on Elba, and he went into a fit of grieving for two days. When he died in 1821, again in exile (this time on Saint Helena), her name was the last word he ever spoke.

In October 1795, a little over a year after the Thermidorian Reaction, which had overthrown Robespierre and the Committee of Public Safety, a mob of royalists, believing the time was ripe to push for a return of the monarchy now that the more radical revolutionaries had been put down, stormed the National Convention. At this time, the members of the convention had been meeting in the same Tuileries Palace where Napoleon had witnessed the mob kill so many of the Royal Guard three years before. Back then, Napoleon was convinced that if the Royal Guard had opened fire with their available artillery, the mob would have dispersed. In 1795, Director Paul Barras ordered Napoleon to put down the royalists. Along with a cavalry officer named Joachim Murat, who would go on to become one of Napoleon's favorite marshals, Napoleon gathered together several large artillery pieces and opened fire on the crowd. An estimated 1,400 people were killed, and the rest of the mob fled. Asked later how he repelled the mob supposedly, Napoleon said, "I gave them a whiff of grapeshot." Grapeshot was essentially smaller cannonballs chained together and piled into the cannon's barrel—think of a *very* large shotgun. Napoleon indeed used grapeshot, but he didn't utter those famous words—they were the words of a later British biographer.

If Napoleon had pulled this stunt a few years earlier, he would, at the very least, have been removed from command and/or sent to a distant post, never to be heard from again. However, he had saved the government of the Directory, suppressed the still unpopular royalists, and, most importantly, after years and years of street violence, had stopped yet another riot before it really started.

The suppression of the royalists propelled Napoleon to national fame. Within days, he was given a promotion to the position of commander of the Interior, a handsome reward and salary, and the protection of the government against any jealous competitors in the army. Soon after, he was given command of the Army of Italy, as the French were embroiled in their efforts to spread revolutionary ideas there. France had also been fighting with the armies of Savoy, Piedmont, and, more importantly, the Empire of Austria, which had great influence in Italy, especially in the northern provinces.

Napoleon's Military Exploits

It is literally no exaggeration to say that more books have been written about Napoleon in the almost two centuries since he lived than almost any other figure in history. There are volumes alone on his relationships with Joséphine, his marshals, his family, his effect on the future of France, his relations with a variety of countries, and more. In all likelihood, most of the books on Napoleon have to do with his military campaigns, victories, and defeats. Books on his defeat at Waterloo in 1815 could fill the libraries of large towns. All that to say that this book is a broad history of France, covering from the time of the earliest cavemen at Lascaux to the post-WWII years. The campaigns and the intricacies of Napoleon's battles would take up the rest of this volume and many more. The people fascinated by Napoleon's battles are, in fact, numberless and exceedingly knowledgeable (and there are also literally thousands of reenactors as well). If you're one of those incredibly knowledgeable people, feel free to skim through this chapter, as you most likely have already learned what's to come next. For those of you who are just getting interested in French history and Napoleon, here is your introduction to the man that many believe is still the greatest general in the history of mankind.

Napoleon certainly was the greatest general of his time. His campaigns were marked by meticulous preparation. When he could, he trained and retrained his troops when others at the time were simply putting men in uniforms and pointing them at the enemy, perhaps giving the men a smattering of practice in formation maneuvers and how to load and care for a musket. That was to change after Napoleon's enemies saw how the fruits of his labor paid off, but in the last years of the 18th century and the first years of the 19th century, the French Army under Napoleon was the best drilled, most practiced, and best led in Europe.

In American football, sometimes a coach comes along that simply "throws away the playbook," meaning he does something completely different than what is expected or is traditional. Napoleon threw away the playbook and wrote his own at the same time. It's as if the Green Bay Packers of the early/mid-1960s had to play against the 49ers of the 80s or the Patriots of the 2000s. They would simply not be in the same league, and that was the case with Napoleon's foes throughout most of his career.

Napoleon's campaigns were marked by speed, surprise, and the uncanny ability to predict his opponent's reactions. He often divided his forces when he was about to face the enemy, something that was seemingly against the unwritten rules of warfare of the time, especially since artillery was just coming into its own. Napoleon played with his enemies after a fashion in this manner, as he realized the importance of keeping one's enemies off-balance.

"The Little Corporal," as enemies often pejoratively referred to him and his men occasionally with fondness, drove his men hard. At first, they resented him for it, but when they realized that it paid off with victory after victory, they realized the importance not only of his hard training but also of speed. Napoleon was often at a place days before his enemies expected him to be there. He would know where his enemy was going to march seemingly before they did. Since he arrived before his enemy, he could choose the most advantageous positions at his leisure. Napoleon himself would often comment that the battle is "often won before the fighting even begins."

Napoleon's rise to fame within France began with Toulon and Tuileries. His fame throughout Europe spread after his first Italian campaign, which lasted from 1796 to 1797. In the late spring of 1796, Napoleon was sent to northern Italy to prevent the Austrians from cementing their power and advancing into France. For almost exactly a year, Napoleon and his generals fought the Austrians in some twenty-six battles. Many of these battles were led by Napoleon himself. In others, his generals, who had been molded to fight according to his ideas, fought to great victories. The French were only held or brought to a stalemate on a couple of occasions. Worse for the Austrians, they frequently outnumbered the French, but they were almost always outmaneuvered and outfought by the forces under Bonaparte.

There are two important points to be made here. Firstly, since the French Revolution, the officer corps of the French Army was made up of men who, for the most part, had talent. During the time of the absolute monarchy, generals were always members of the nobility, as were virtually all the officers. A few were excellent, some were good, and many were awful. With the changes brought about by the revolution, officers were promoted, for the most part, on talent. This was accelerated under Napoleon, as a number of his commanders had begun their military careers as non-commissioned officers (corporals and sergeants). It was made clear in Italy that Napoleon earned the loyalty of his men. This was particularly true at the Battle of Lodi ("loh-dee") in northern Italy. At Lodi, the French were forced to cross a bridge under heavy fire from the Austrians holding it and the opposite bank. It was a bloody affair, and it cost the French dearly, but after a number of attacks, bravely led by highly ranked French officers, the Austrians were forced to retreat. It is said that Napoleon himself directed the fire of the French guns near the bridge, assuming the role of corporal for himself and placing himself in danger. From then on, many of his veterans referred to him as the "Little Corporal" with great fondness, for it was apparent that he would not refuse to do what he asked of his soldiers.

During this time, Napoleon set up the Ligurian Republic and the Cisalpine Republic in northern Italy, basing them on French revolutionary ideas. Though he did set up representative assemblies in these territories, for a time, Napoleon ruled behind the scenes, alarming many in the Directory who asked themselves if they had created a monster that might do away with them.

In October 1797, Napoleon and the Austrians signed the Treaty of Campo Formio. According to the terms, France would receive the Austrian Netherlands (today's Belgium), and Austria would recognize the Cisalpine and Ligurian Republics. The Cisalpine Republic would control all of Lombardy (most of northwestern Italy), and the French would also be given Austrian territory east of the Rhine River and a number of Greek islands under Austrian control. Austria would, in turn, receive control of the Italian lands on the east coast of the Adriatic, which makes up much of today's Croatia.

By taking control of the Austrian Netherlands and the left bank of the Rhine, the French, thanks to Napoleon Bonaparte, had regained what had always been believed to be the "natural borders" of France, what they had been first under Charlemagne and then under Louis XIV.

Egypt

When Napoleon returned to France, he received a hero's welcome, but there were many, both in power and on the street, who were becoming wary of the Corsican general. He had an army that was seemingly only loyal to him, and he had exceeded his authority in both forming and running the Cisalpine and Ligurian Republics. Though in the end, the establishment of these lands was good for France (or so it was thought), and the Treaty of Campo Formio had "restored" France's "natural borders." However, Napoleon had also acquired tremendous wealth. Both he and his troops enriched themselves on the lands they conquered. For his troops, it was food, whatever riches they could seize, and the age-old terror of rape and thuggery without consequence. For Napoleon, it was much more. He did send large amounts of treasure back to France (this was how France financed its wars, which meant that, in order to keep the people happy at home, more wars and more plunder were needed), but he also enriched himself at the same time. Banks, local governments, art, and much more were added to Napoleon's personal coffers.

The combination of intelligence and charisma, a loyal army, and wealth made Napoleon a dangerous man for those in power. The Directory itself owed its survival to Napoleon for destroying the royalist mob that was bent on restoring the old order in 1795. He and other generals also sent troops to aid the Directors in removing royalists from the two legislative houses of government in September 1797, which added to his influence. Napoleon was growing in power, and everyone knew it. And if they didn't, they could find out in the two newspapers he established.

However, in October 1797, when the Treaty of Campo Formio was signed, Napoleon was not prepared to seize power, nor is it exactly clear when he began to think of placing himself at the head of the French state. For now, he was satisfied with a new task: planning the invasion of England.

Though England had a relatively small (but growing) army, its navy was second to none. Ever since the defeat of the Spanish Armada in 1588, England's navy continued to grow, bringing English power, influence, commerce, and colonists to almost every corner of the globe. Worse yet, England's position across the English Channel (there's a reason it's called the "English Channel" and not the "French Channel") made her a direct threat to France's coastal cities, its commerce, and any potential navy it might develop. The Directors, like the radical revolutionaries and the long list of French kings before them, were determined to do something about it.

However, after two months of careful study, Napoleon reported to the government that in its current state, neither the government, its treasury, and its forces were in a position to undertake a cross-Channel invasion of the British Isles. The best the French could do was to harass the British wherever possible until they were able to launch an invasion. The French sent money and arms to rebels in Ireland, and it fought a series of naval battles with the English in the West Indies, most of which did not go well.

The Directory was in agreement with Napoleon's conclusions and then supported his idea to harass the English at another point: Egypt. Napoleon's goal was to seize Egypt, which was then ruled by the Muslim Mamluk dynasty, and prevent English trade from going across land to the Red Sea and then to India by ship, where the English were establishing themselves as a power. He also hoped to defeat the Mamluks and, like his hero Alexander the Great, push on to India and take British possessions and influence for himself. This would also serve as a way to get Napoleon far from the center of power in France.

Though Napoleon won great victories over the Mamluks and took control over the richest part of Egypt, in doing so, his troops suffered tremendously from heat, disease, and thirst. Many literally lost their minds and wandered off to their deaths in the desert. The French fleet that had transported Napoleon and his army was also defeated by the man who would become one of England's greatest heroes and Napoleon's nemesis, Admiral Horatio Nelson. Nelson's fleet almost completely destroyed the French at the Battle of the Nile in August 1798, leaving but a handful of French ships afloat.

The Egyptian campaign was a disaster for Napoleon, even though he did not lose a battle on land. His army was decimated mostly from heat and disease, especially from the plague, and the British had destroyed his lifeline to Europe and any additional supplies. In July 1799, Napoleon left Egypt, bringing back some wounded men but leaving most of his army behind. The survivors were repatriated to France in 1801 by agreement with the English, who had defeated the remnants of Napoleon's army there.

Coup of 18 Brumaire, Year VIII

Napoleon returned to France without permission, but the Directory had already sent orders for him to return, which he never received. While Napoleon was away, the situation in France was dire, as France's enemies, which at this point consisted of England, Austria, Russia, and a smattering of lesser powers, including Portugal, Sweden, and a number of German states, had won victory after victory from 1798 to 1799. When Bonaparte returned to Paris, the military situation had stabilized, but the political one was in flux.

The Directory was hated. It was seen as corrupt, which it was, and ineffective, which it was to a great degree, especially in dealing with economic problems. Inflation was perhaps the biggest issue, which terrified both the French people and the government, as inflation had been one of the prime movers behind the French Revolution in 1789.

When Napoleon returned, he was given a hero's welcome. Although the campaign was a failure, he successfully played up his own victories and blamed the campaign's defeats and problems on others. At the same time, Napoleon also entered into a plot with a number of influential politicians to overthrow the government of the Directory. Napoleon was involved with the famous Abbé Sieyès, who had been a powerful clergyman and early supporter of the revolution); Sieyès's brother, Lucien, the speaker of the lower house of the French assembly (the Council of the Five Hundred); another Director named Joseph Fouché; and Charles-Maurice de Talleyrand (better known as just "Talleyrand"), who was the ultimate survivor, as he had gone from royalist to revolutionary to supporter. He later became the foreign minister under Napoleon and then served the succeeding French government after Bonaparte was gone. These men formed a group bent on overthrowing the Directory and installing themselves as the new power.

This coup occurred on November 9th, 1799 (18th Brumaire by the revolutionary calendar, which is how the event is known to history and historians). Napoleon and the others arranged for the two assemblies (the Council of the Five Hundred and the Council of Ancients) to be moved to another location because of a supposed threat from royalists. Napoleon gave a speech to the assembled representatives in which he poorly attempted to explain what was going on. Many of the men began to heckle and shout him down, and the coup was on the verge of failing when Napoleon's friend and deputy, General Murat, showed up with a contingent of troops. Under threat, the legislators agreed on a new constitution, which was presented to them the next morning and which called for a new form of government known as the Consulate.

Illustration 34: General Bonaparte in the Council of the Five Hundred, at Saint-Cloud, 10 November 1799, *by François Bouchot, 1840.*

Surprising his fellow plotters, Napoleon named himself the first consul. Abbé Sieyès and the others had to accept this; after all, Napoleon had control of the troops in Paris. As the first consul, Napoleon had the power to appoint the *Conseil d'État* (the "Council of State"), which was given the power to draft laws and appoint army officers, judges, ambassadors, and ministers of state. The three new (mostly "rubber-stamp") legislative chambers were the Tribunat, the Corps législatif, and the Sénat.

What did the people of France think of this radical new change? Generally speaking, the change was welcome. The Directory, as stated, was corrupt and unpopular. The people had been through over ten years of revolution marked by political violence, civil war, and war with enemies outside of France. They wanted stability and order, and Napoleon and his fellow consuls promised both.

The years of the Consulate saw a great change in France and the continued rise of Napoleon's popularity. Napoleon oversaw tremendous changes in the way France was governed, much of which remains in place today. Administratively, France was organized as departments, which were large administrative bodies akin to American states but more closely tied to the central government. Napoleon handpicked *préfets* ("prefects") as regional governors, who were answerable to him, and reformed the civil service. Famously, he instituted France's highest honor, the *Légion d'honneur* ("Legion of Honor"), for both civilians and military, stating that both had an important role to play in the life of the state. Both of these Napoleonic changes are in place today, albeit with some minor changes.

Napoleon also undertook a new program of infrastructure, improving roads, canals, and tunnels for improved and faster transportation, as well as improvements in sewage and public health. The changes were immensely popular in France, and as the period of the Consulate went on (1799–1804), people clearly saw that it was Napoleon who was responsible for the changes.

Perhaps Napoleon's most famous non-military achievement was also installed at this time. This was the *Code Napoléon* ("Napoleonic Code"), the system of laws which bears his name and which he had a great deal of influence over. Many people believe that the Napoleonic Code was actually written by Bonaparte himself—it was not. He formed a commission that met some eighty times to complete the project. Napoleon was present at over half of them.

The *Code Napoléon* codified many of the existing laws of varying regions of France in one place and eliminated those thought to be ineffective, unjust, or outdated. It broke the law down into branches—commercial, criminal, and civil—and further broke down civil law into property and family law.

One of the more unpopular parts of the code, at least among the progressive and revolutionary-minded women of Paris, was its return to the old laws under the monarchs regarding the role of women. The right of women to vote was taken away, and it also took away many of their individual rights, especially in regards to marriage.

Equally distressing from the point of view of the radical revolutionaries of the 1790s was the reintroduction of slavery in France's colonies in the New World, which gave rise to revolts of all kinds, especially and most famously in Haiti.

On the positive side, the equality of all men under the law was recognized. During this time, the majority of European countries still counted the word and deeds of noblemen far above those of commoners, so this was groundbreaking. Religious freedom and the freedom to dissent were also guaranteed.

As you can imagine, the actions of Napoleon and his co-conspirators did not go completely unopposed. Both ends of the political spectrum, royalists on the right, who saw Napoleon attempting to create a new type of monarchy and replacing the old

Bourbon royal family, and radicals on the left, who saw exactly the same thing but were opposed to it for far different reasons.

On Christmas Eve, 1800, Napoleon and Joséphine were on their way to the Paris opera house. Because of scheduling, they were riding in different carriages, but they were not far from each other as they rode down the crowded boulevard. As they neared the opera house, a wagon loaded with barrels of gunpowder was pushed down the road and glided in between them. The distance between the carriages of Napoleon, Joséphine, and crude but powerful "infernal machine" (as Napoleon would later call it) was enough so that when the explosives went off, the intended target and his wife were unharmed. However, fifty-two people were killed or wounded, including Joséphine's step-daughter, who was wounded in the wrist. After surveying the scene, Napoleon insisted on going to the opera, where he was greeted with a standing ovation.

The perpetrators of the Plot of the rue Saint-Nicaise, named for the street where the bomb exploded, was the job of staunchly Catholic royalist supporters who wanted a return of the old monarchy and the former preeminence of the Catholic Church.

Amazingly, Napoleon blamed the attempt on his life on the remains of the radical Jacobins. Though his co-consul Joseph Fouché knew that the plot was the product of royalists, he went along with Bonaparte's thoughts, and the two staged an elaborate trial of 130 Jacobins, who were exiled from France. Four of the actual perpetrators (those who constructed and provided materials for the bomb) were guillotined, and their ties to royalist financiers were downplayed. Napoleon believed the radical left was a greater danger to his rule than the royalists, whom he planned to deal with in another way. Another result of the assassination attempt was the further development of the secret police and informer system, which had begun during the Terror and were increased by Napoleon until France became as close to a police state as possible with the limited technology of the 1800s.

Italian Campaign Part II

France's two prime enemies, Austria and England, were not prepared to make peace with a new type of French revolutionary government headed by a man who clearly had aspirations of grandiosity. France was still the largest, most populous, and richest country on the Continent, complete with the biggest army.

England's goal was not necessarily the complete defeat of France but rather making sure that she was not so powerful as to threaten England's dominance of the sea and commercial interests on land. If Napoleon and France were defeated, so be it, but from this time until the dawn of WWII, the British would seek a "balance of power" in Europe to prevent the dominance of one nation or nations over the others.

The Austrians, on the other hand, were still stung from the many defeats that Napoleon had inflicted upon them in his first Italian campaign (1796–1797), so they were eager to both defeat him and regain their influence in Italy and in Europe in general. Joining the Austrians was a sizable Russian force, which inflicted a defeat on the French at Novi in the Piedmont region of Italy. However, after this, the Russians were diverted to face the French Army threatening Switzerland, and they didn't play another significant role in the campaign.

Illustration 35: Napoleon Crossing the Alps *or* Napoleon at the Saint-Bernard Pass *(1801) by Jacques-Louis David. This is perhaps the most famous painting of Bonaparte and an early example of political propaganda. There were five versions of the painting done by the artist with various changes in colors. Note the names engraved on the rocks at the bottom: Hannibal and Caesar.*

Napoleon's second Italian campaign (also known as the War of the Second Coalition to historians) went much as the first did, with Napoleon thoroughly dominating the Austrians on land, despite them receiving British aid in the form of naval blockades and coastal attacks. There were many battles and sieges, both large and small, in this campaign, which lasted from 1799 to 1800, but the most significant was at Marengo, Italy, in June 1800. Marengo was a close call for Napoleon, whose outnumbered forces were almost defeated. The late arrival of French cavalry, which had been sent to reconnoiter another part of the area, saved Napoleon's forces from a major loss.

With their arrival and quick thinking and maneuvering by Bonaparte, Marengo and one final French victory at Hohenlinden in southern Germany forced the Austrians to make peace with Napoleon once again. The Treaty of Lunéville gave more Italian territory to France and forced Austria out of the war. Within a year,

Britain signed a peace treaty with Bonaparte, and for one year, Europe enjoyed peace. It was to be the only period of peace in Europe from 1793 to 1814.

The Concordat

In 1801, Napoleon reached out to Pope Pius VII in an attempt to reconcile France with the Catholic Church. Ever since the French Revolution, the church had watched its power, wealth, and influence over the French wane. Despite its waning power and influence, the church was still an important institution in France, and despite the attempts of the revolutionaries to remove it from French life, the hold of the Catholic Church on the people's hearts was still strong everywhere but Paris and some of the other larger cities. At times and in some places, devout Catholics and clergy had to hold their services in secret and be very circumspect about their beliefs, but the people still held on to their traditions, feast days, and saints. Napoleon knew this, and he also knew that if he could come to an arrangement with the pope, he might gain even more support in the country.

This proved true. With the Concordat of 1801, France and the Catholic Church reconciled. The agreement was extremely one-sided. Napoleon controlled the outcome from the start, and he essentially dictated the terms of the document to the pope's representatives. The pope wanted, or perhaps hoped is a better word, that the church might gain back most or at least some of the lands and tax privileges it had lost in the early days of the revolution. This was not to be. Napoleon wanted the support of the French Catholics, who had not supported him up to this point, but he was never going to give the church back the power, wealth, and privilege it had enjoyed before 1789. That would not only threaten his position but also infuriate the people who had given so much since 1789 to reduce the power of the church and nobility.

Napoleon also retained the right to name or approve French bishops. Of course, Napoleon would appoint people who were loyal to him, not to Rome. The government would pay the clergy, not the church. Napoleon announced that the government recognized that most French people were Catholic, but he did not name Catholicism the state religion as it had once been and as the pope wanted. He also asserted the rights of minority religions, expressly Protestantism and Judaism.

For its part, the church could name priests and other clergymen, and holy days, such as Easter, were recognized as festival days in France once again.

As you can see, Napoleon got much while the church received little, but it was enough for the pope at the time, whose alternative was nothing. For his part, Napoleon kept control of the church in government hands while at the same time pleasing most of the French Catholics, who could now worship without worry and be recognized as the majority in France.

In January 1804, another assassination plot against Napoleon was uncovered by the secret police, which was supposed to have been headed by the Bourbon family, which was represented by the duke of Enghien (Louis XVI's godson), who resided in Baden, Germany. Theoretically, he was out of Bonaparte's reach, but he soon found out that he wasn't as safe as he thought. Napoleon had the duke kidnapped and brought to France, where he was held incommunicado for two months. He was then supposedly brought to trial and executed on Napoleon's orders. This action alarmed the crowned heads of Europe, especially Tsar Alexander I of Russia, who, at least for a while, was determined to remove Napoleon from power.

This plot, along with others, assured Napoleon that he needed to take the final step to solidify his power. Back in 1802, he had held an election. On it was one question: "Should Napoleon Bonaparte be made Consul for Life?" He won 99 percent of the non-secret ballot, but he likely would have won a secret ballot as well. In November 1804, another open plebiscite (a vote on one issue) cemented Napoleon as the emperor of the French.

Illustration 36: The Coronation of Napoleon
by *Jacques-Louis David (1805-1807).*

In the painting above, it appears that Napoleon is about to crown himself, and indeed he did. He already had a Roman-style olive-leaf crown upon his head, which he then removed and crowned himself with, parting with the tradition of French kings, all of whom had been crowned by the pope. It was very obvious that Bonaparte was signaling that, at least in France and its empire, he, not the pope, was the ultimate power. The date was December 2nd, 1804. Some months later, he was also crowned as the king of Italy. Within a short time, he had begun establishing a new nobility, lavishing titles and properties on those loyal to him or to those he thought useful.

Throughout Europe, rulers were alarmed. First came the French Revolution, then the Reign of Terror, and now Napoleon was the emperor of the French and anointed by the pope. Since 1789, many of the kingdoms of Europe had experienced upheavals of varying degrees by those who were inspired by revolutionary ideals. Napoleon establishing himself as an emperor, which is greater than a king, did not calm things. He had shown that certain

Enlightenment ideals could exist at least somewhat peacefully with a new type of royalty. Worse still, perhaps, was the idea that no matter under what name or guise, the crowned heads of Europe could be replaced. And a seemingly invincible military genius was the one to test the waters.

1805 and the Third Coalition

The story of Napoleon Bonaparte is long and remarkable. He had risen from a bullied foreigner to the emperor of France. He crowned himself at the age of thirty-five. He had won every battle where he was present. He even changed the course of American history by selling French possessions on the North American continent to the United States in the famed Louisiana Purchase. In 1804, he was back at war with England and much of Europe. In 1805, he would win his greatest victory at Austerlitz.

In the spring of 1803, the British broke the Treaty of Amiens, which had been signed in 1802 to bring an end to the wars of the revolutionary period and redraw boundaries, and once again declared war on a France that was gaining too much power in Europe. By 1805, the kingdoms of Sweden, Russia, and Austria formed the Third Coalition against France.

England had ample reason for declaring war on Napoleon, prime of which was his building up of an invasion force on the French side of the Channel. The story of Napoleon's *Armée d'Angleterre* ("Army of England") is a huge and interesting topic in and of itself, but suffice it to say that Bonaparte assembled over 200,000 men and began building a huge fleet of transports to move his men, horses, and cannons to England to eliminate what he rightly perceived as the greatest threat to his power.

Between May and July of 1805, Napoleon seriously planned for the invasion of England. His plan hinged on a bold idea for part of his navy to break out of their English-blockaded ports and threaten England's valuable possessions in the West Indies. At the same time, another group of French vessels, combined with an allied fleet of Spanish warships, would break into the English Channel and escort his invasion fleet across the Channel.

The idea collapsed for two reasons. Firstly, the main Franco-Spanish fleet was defeated at the Battle of Cape Finisterre in July. Secondly, though a brilliant general on land, Napoleon was forced to cede command to his naval commanders, and both they and the French fleet were nowhere near capable of challenging or defeating the British Royal Navy. Most historians believe that even had the French fleet been able to move into the Channel, they would have been able to only cover the invasion force for all of about two minutes—that's how powerful the Royal Navy was at the time. And even had they been able to move troops swiftly across the Channel, the Royal Navy would have swiftly taken control of that body of water, and the French troops in England would've been stranded and defeated.

Not only had the French Navy been defeated and hemmed in, but by late summer, Napoleon's European enemies were marching westward. One great advantage that came out of his troops' time on the coast was the amazing amount of training they received while waiting for the word to invade. By the summer, the veteran officers and sergeants had whipped his new army into a fighting force that was more highly trained and motivated than any he had commanded before. La Grande Armée of 1805 was the greatest fighting force in the world, and it was led by the best general the world may have ever seen. He was joined by commanders who had, due to the changes brought about by the revolution, risen by ability rather than birth or connections.

At the beginning of September, Napoleon began marching his army toward the Rhine River, where he expected to meet the enemy's forces. At a time when troops traveled mainly on foot, Bonaparte's forces traveled both quickly and with relative secrecy toward France's natural border with the German states.

The resulting Ulm campaign showed Napoleon at his most brilliant. He outmaneuvered a massive Austrian force at the city of Ulm, and in a series of battles, he both defeated and outmaneuvered them back toward their capital of Vienna. In November, he captured the famed and beautiful Austrian capital.

Among the residents of the city was Ludwig van Beethoven, who, in 1803, had begun his Third Symphony and named it "Bonaparte" for the ideals of equality and religious freedom that he believed Napoleon symbolized. By the time the composer was finished with the work, he had changed both its dedication and its name, for Napoleon had named himself emperor in what Beethoven and many other liberals in Europe saw as a betrayal. The Third Symphony has borne the name *Eroica* (*Heroic*) since that time.

Illustration 37: The frontispiece to Beethoven's Third Symphony with the composer's violent scratching out of Napoleon's name.

The capture of Vienna not only conferred glory and riches on Napoleon and his army but also supplied him with massive numbers of captured cannons, muskets, and ammunition. Both Emperor Francis II of Austria and Tsar Alexander I of Russia were eager to retrieve Vienna from the French. Despite counsel from many of their generals that fighting Napoleon in winter when their armies were still stunned from prior defeats was a mistake, the Austrians and Russians moved to engage Napoleon, and the armies came together at Austerlitz, in today's Czech Republic, on December 2nd, 1805.

Even Napoleon, who had an incredible self-regard about his abilities and performance on the battlefield, later said that the Battle of Austerlitz was his "finest" moment, and most military historians agree with him. The battle was a masterpiece of maneuver, feint, speed, and decisive action. Napoleon rightly gets most of the credit for the outcome of the battle, but his marshals performed perfectly as well.

Out of a force of roughly 85,000 to 95,000 men, the Austrians and Russians lost perhaps 16,000 killed and wounded. Twenty thousand were likely captured. More than a third of their armies were eliminated in one way or another. The French lost comparatively few: just over 1,000 men killed, 7,000 wounded, and under 600 captured. The Austrians and Russians were forced to sue for peace, and in the Peace of Pressburg, Napoleon once again confirmed his control of former Austrian lands in Italy. The Austrian-controlled states in Germany were given to both France and Napoleon's German allies (prime of which was Bavaria). Most importantly, Napoleon gained an indemnity of *forty million* gold francs (likely more than one billion in today's US dollars). In return, Russian troops were allowed free passage back to Russia. (If you are interested in learning more about Austerlitz, there is an outstanding and highly detailed history of the battle in the reference section at the end of this book.)

Only one thing prevented Napoleon from his greatest prize, which was total victory over his enemies, especially Great Britain. This was the French Navy's defeat at the Battle of Trafalgar on October 21st, 1805, during which time he was involved in the Ulm campaign. The British defeat of the French fleet off the coast of Spain meant that Napoleon would never again dream of being able to challenge the British at sea, even with the death of its greatest hero, Admiral Horatio Nelson, who died at Trafalgar. Napoleon would have to find another way to bring England to the negotiating table or, more preferably, to its knees.

The Continental System and the Peninsular War

In 1806 and again in 1807, Napoleon announced that none of his allies or subject countries were to trade with England and its colonies or in English goods. Failure to follow this, what he called the Continental System, would result in greater taxation, looting, and the possible installation of more France-friendly governments.

On the surface of it, it appeared that the Continental System might actually work. Napoleon had the troops guard much of western Europe's coasts and a fleet big enough to challenge unescorted trading vessels or smaller English naval groups. However, Europe is a large continent. By this time, England had established a worldwide trading network. England also had three distinct advantages: its huge navy, the demand for English goods in Europe (England was at the forefront of the Industrial Revolution, turning out massive quantities of refined goods and raw materials from its colonies, especially coffee and spices), and Portugal.

Portugal had been an English ally since the early 1700s. This was primarily because English ships could protect Portugal's large overseas trade from Spain and protect its territory from the Spanish Army. This overseas trade was established in the 1500s/1600s in the Age of Discovery when Portugal had a powerful fleet. Portugal also had a long coastline, which allowed British goods to enter Europe. These goods could (and were) smuggled through Spain into Europe and the Mediterranean.

By 1807, Napoleon had had enough. Convinced that the Spanish were tacitly allowing British goods through their country, Napoleon sent an army of nearly 100,000 men into Spain. By the next year, through a series of political maneuvers that only angered the Spanish more, Napoleon first displaced the mentally ill Spanish king with a noble loyal to Bonaparte, then replaced him with his own brother, Joseph Bonaparte, who became the king of Spain.

Spain had been a divided country. Many supported the king even though he was seriously deranged. Spain was not France, so the Catholic Church played a regular and, some might say, oppressive role in the ruling and life of the country. The Spanish Catholic Church, which had been somewhat independent of Rome for centuries, hated Napoleon and the French revolutionary ideals he brought with his armies. And then, of course, there were the French armies, which soon began to treat Spain as their own bank, farm, and other unpleasant things.

Over the course of the next few years, Napoleon's troops were not able to gain control of the country. This was due to British armies arriving in Spain, the British navy making it impossible to travel quickly from France to Spain by sea (they had to take the overland route across the rugged Pyrenees Mountains instead), and, probably most decisively, the Spanish, many of whom formed into the first "guerrilla" bands in history. "Guerrilla" means "little war," and the Spanish, knowing they could not engage the French in open battle, harassed French troops whenever they could. They participated in assassinations, attacked French supply columns when the advantage was theirs, isolated French bases, and poisoned wells. Everything that typified guerrilla warfare in the 20th century, in places like Vietnam, essentially began in Spain in the early 1800s.

Illustration 38: Francisco Goya's famous The Third of May 1808 *depicts the massacre of Spanish civilians at the hands of frustrated and enraged French troops during the beginning of the guerrilla war.*

The war in Spain was made worse with the intervention of relatively large numbers of British troops, which were still far fewer than the French. In precisely chosen battles to taken advantage of the French having to occupy most of the country, the British and Portuguese, led by a soon-to-be-famous English general named Arthur Wellesley (or, as he is known to history for the role he played in finally defeating Napoleon, Lord Wellington), inflicted defeats on the French. Eventually, Napoleon himself arrived after securing his rear flank in Europe with negotiations with Austria, which was in no shape to fight again, though they were rapidly retraining their troops, and Russia, with which Napoleon agreed he would do nothing if they took over Finland. Once there, Napoleon pushed the English out of the Spanish Peninsula in 1808 by winning the Battle of Corunna.

However, Napoleon could not remain on a campaign in Spain indefinitely. In 1808, the British sent another army to Spain, where they, their Spanish guerrilla allies, and the Portuguese waged a long, drawn-out conflict with the French, whose troops eventually numbered over 300,000 in Spain. After Napoleon's defeat in Russia in 1812, that number declined rapidly. Some historians believe that if Napoleon had not been bogged down in Spain, he might have had the extra troops he needed to fend off the Russians in 1812.

1809 – Austria, Again, and Tilsit

In April 1809, the newly trained and equipped Austrian army marched out to do battle with Napoleon yet again. This campaign, Bonaparte's fourth against the Austrians, was the hardest fought of them all. He suffered a stunning defeat at Essling (a case of over-confidence and a rare lack of tactical thinking on Napoleon's part), but he was able to impose a harsh peace on the Austrians after a bloody victory at Wagram in late May. Austria lost its territories in Poland, the Adriatic Coast opposite Italy, and other territories.

Back in 1806, Napoleon had defeated the forces of the strongest German state, Prussia, and had inflicted defeat on the Russians at Friedland in 1807. Alexander I decided to make the best of a bad situation and came to an agreement with France to take advantage of Austria's weakness while it had the chance.

At Tilsit (in today's small Russian possession of Kaliningrad on the Baltic Coast), the two emperors met on an elaborate raft in the middle of the Niemen River. Over the course of several days in July 1807, the two men talked on a variety of subjects. Alexander I was apparently in awe of Napoleon, and for his part, Napoleon seemed to like the Russian. The result of the talks was the creation of several French satellite kingdoms in Germany and Poland (some of which were ruled by Napoleon's brothers). In return, Russia received the rest of Austria's possessions in Poland, agreed to join the Continental System, and agreed to hand over some Russian-controlled territories in the Balkans. For that, Napoleon granted safety to the tsar's cousins, who ruled various smaller German states.

Personal Life

In December 1809, Napoleon divorced the love of his life, Joséphine. The reason? She was unable to bear him children. He was in love with her to the end of his days, but by this point, he was becoming concerned with the continuation of his dynasty. He cast about the royal families of Europe, looking for an eligible princess. He even talked with Alexander I about marrying one of his sisters. Alexander was all for this, hoping the marriage might forestall or prevent war between Russia and France, but this fell through to Alexander's consternation. Napoleon ended up marrying the Austrian princess Marie Louise of the Habsburg family, daughter of Francis I, Emperor of Austria and Bonaparte's arch-enemy. It was hoped the marriage would secure peace between the two powers.

Marie Louise gave Napoleon one son, Napoléon François Joseph Charles Bonaparte, who was given the title "King of Rome" at birth. The marriage was not popular in France—if you remember, King Louis XVI's wife, Marie Antoinette, was Austrian and the new empress's great-aunt. Joséphine remained popular in France, however, and kept her estates. She was given the title "Empress Dowager."

Russia

In the years between the Treaty of Tilsit (1807) and 1810, Russia aligned itself, to a degree, with Napoleon. It adhered, at least officially, to the Continental System against England and refrained from military activities outside of its borders. One reason for this was Napoleon's power. Another was the position of England, which was allied with Sweden. Sweden and Russia were long-time enemies, and in this case, the saying "the enemy of my enemy is my friend" held true.

However, at the Congress of Erfurt in 1808, Napoleon and his satellite nations, along with Russia, met to pound out a European foreign policy. Though Russia was a mighty power itself, with the largest land empire in the world, it was, at the time, second fiddle to Napoleon militarily, especially in Europe. As a result, Napoleon treated it and its tsar as such.

Between 1808 and 1810, the Russians began to slowly move away from Napoleon, and in 1810, Tsar Alexander I broke with Napoleon and announced that he would be dealing economically with England once again. The reasons were many, but primarily, any nation that had joined the economic embargo with France against England was subject to English naval blockade, seizure, or even action. Since the majority of Russian trade went through the Baltic Sea and out into the North Sea/Atlantic Ocean, where the Royal Navy was strongest, its agreement with France began to take an economic toll on Russia. In addition, England was in the beginning stages of its second period of colonialism, which would see it carve out the largest empire in the history of man. Already, the countries bordering Russia, such as Persia, Afghanistan, and nearby India, were feeling English pressure, as were the Ottoman Turks in the Middle East. Russia was being hemmed in, and it was partially doing it to itself.

Napoleon, for both personal and political reasons, could not let Russia back out of the Continental System. For one, his image would be tarnished in France and Europe. Personally, Napoleon was not the kind of person one said "no" to, and he could not accept that someone had. Politically and economically, allowing goods into Russia would strengthen England and possibly encourage others to join or at least trade with the British.

Sometime after Alexander I's announcement, Napoleon decided to invade Russia. This was no simple proposition, at least logistically. It would involve over a thousand miles (more if you consider detours) and an amazing number of men, horses, food, cannons, ammunition, clothing, etc. As we have seen, Napoleon was a mathematical genius. Napoleon was going to bring his largest army yet (500,000 men) to Russia, and he knew almost to a "T" exactly what they would need, at least under perfect circumstances.

Interestingly enough, though, while Napoleon was thinking about war with Russia, Russia and its leader were acting on the idea of a war with France. Aside from the issue of the Continental System, Russia had deep concerns about Napoleon's division of the Duchy of Warsaw (most of modern-day Poland) and his placement of Frederick Augustus I of Saxony as the head of the duchy. Poland and Russia had been enemies for centuries, and in 1772, Austria, Prussia, and Russia divided the country between themselves in a local "balance of power." Lastly, the Russians were upset at the French emperor's annexation of the German Duchy of Oldenburg, which contained a major port on the North Sea. Though this was just a pretext, Alexander I used the French move as an excuse to declare war on France.

The problem with Russia was that it was not western or even eastern Europe. Settlements, towns, and cities were far apart, and the lands between them were sometimes just open plains that were exposed to the worst of the weather. Even at that time, the road system in mainland Europe, especially in France, Germany, Belgium, and Austria, was relatively good. In and near large cities, they were many times paved with cobblestones. Even outside the main cities, many of the roads were cared for and were passable except in the absolute worst weather.

This was not so in Russia. Aside from the obvious issues in winter, in both fall and spring, there is a time called the *Rasputitsa* ("the sea of mud"). In the fall, rain causes it, and in the spring, the thaw causes it. A literal "sea of mud" is what it is, as you can see in the picture below of German soldiers experiencing it more than a century later.

Illustration 39: This is 1941. In 1812, there were horses to help pull through the mud. It is certainly unpleasant either way.

Historians or TV pundits on bad history documentaries will sometimes say that neither Napoleon nor Hitler knew it could get cold in Russia. But, of course, they knew, at least theoretically. The problem wasn't that they didn't know as much as they didn't care. Both dictators also expected a quick victory. Hitler expected the Soviets to fold completely in 1941 and cede most of the western part of the country to him. Napoleon, on the other hand, did not have illusions about occupying Russia. He would move into the country and inflict a decisive defeat or two on the Russians, who would then sue for peace, pay a large indemnity, and then toe the Napoleonic line. The problem is he didn't inflict that decisive defeat, which means the Russians didn't sue for peace.

Napoleon moved into Russia in June 1812, two months after the Russian declaration of war. As they would more than a century later against Hitler, the Russians traded space for time. They would not engage Napoleon in any sort of decisive way. This was done for a number of reasons. First, they knew they could not match Napoleon on equal terms or on the ground of his choosing, as they were aware that Napoleon was a master of maneuvering his opponents into just the position he wanted them to be. Second, the Russian army was really no match for the French forces, at least not the majority of it. Many of the French soldiers were well-trained veterans, while many Russians were untrained peasants.

However, Alexander and his marshals (the most famous being Mikhail Kutuzov) knew that Napoleon would not likely do the smart thing and leave Russia once he realized the Russians were giving ground. He would move onto the capital, which was, at this time, Moscow, and hope the tsar would sue for peace then.

The Russians were not going to give their ancient capital to Napoleon without a fight, and in the savage battle of Borodino outside the city, the two sides fought to a bloody stalemate. The Russians eventually left Napoleon in charge of the field. He entered Moscow during the second week of September when there was already a nip in the air. The French hoped that Moscow would provide them with enough supplies and shelter to last through the winter, but soon after entering the city, Moscow went up in flames.

The Russians had not only stripped virtually anything of use from the city, such as food, fuel, ammunition, horses, wagons, and clothing, but they had also set it on fire after removing many of the most valuable items of the royal family. The entire city did not burn as many believe, but enough of it did to present a real problem for the French.

By the middle of October, Napoleon knew he had to leave. His marshals had been pressing him to leave earlier, but he held out until he could no longer reasonably hope to remain any longer. The weather had already turned, and it was going to get worse. By the time Napoleon's army reached the Berezina River in today's Belarus a month later, the troops were starving, their clothes were falling apart, and the breeches on their guns and remaining cannons were freezing solid. Worse still, the Russian army, especially its Cossack cavalry, attacked the edges of the main French force incessantly and then retreated before a counterattack could be organized. On top of this, peasant guerillas began to prey on the French. Illness and starvation killed thousands, as did frostbite. Horses were eaten along with anything found in the abandoned homes along the way.

As they entered the Polish frontier, Napoleon received word of a possible coup d'état in Paris and rode on ahead with his personal guard. The rest of his army froze and starved. Of the 500,000 men he brought with him, only *20,000* returned to France. The Russians had defeated Napoleon, but they were not led by any cunning man. Instead, their victory was due to the famous "General Winter," who made it the worst winter in one hundred years. "He" would do the same in 1941.

Illustration 40: Russian pre-WWI cartoon of "General Winter," the Russian weather that protects the homeland from invaders.

Napoleon faced unrest when he returned to France, but the force of his personality, his glorious past, and his police kept him in power. But by 1813, the Spanish and English had driven the French out of Spain, from which Napoleon had taken 100,000 troops for Russia. Also, in 1813, his other enemies, especially the English and Austrians, who were now joined by the Prussians, Swedes, and Russians, engaged his depleted veterans and ill-trained new recruits in the Battle of Leipzig in Germany, sometimes known as the Battle of the Nations. This defeat forced Napoleon to return to France, and in March 1814, the forces of his many enemies entered Paris.

Napoleon's marshals and others came to him, telling him that he had to abdicate or there would be wholesale slaughter or a popular revolt against him. Napoleon conceded to their wishes and, by the Treaty of Fontainebleau, agreed to live in exile on the island of Elba, off the Mediterranean coast of Italy. He was actually given the right to rule the island, which he set himself to almost as soon as he got there. However, his Austrian wife and his only son left for Austria, and he never saw them again.

For the Allies, the problem of Napoleon was over—at least the man himself. They still had to decide what would happen to his former empire, and they set about doing this at the famous Congress of Vienna (November 1814–June 1815). One of their first decisions was to restore the Bourbon monarchy to France. Louis XVI's brother, now Louis XVIII, was put on the throne. There were grumblings, but after two decades of war and a promise that France would be a constitutional monarchy, things returned to something approaching normal.

While the European powers began to decide on a new conservative order in Europe and to limit the power of France, Napoleon was making plans.

The Hundred Days

Of all the comebacks in history, Napoleon's may have been the greatest, though it was short-lived. On March 1ˢᵗ, 1815, Napoleon secretly boarded a small ship with his staff and the small contingent of soldiers he was allowed to retain. His destination was the southern French coast. He slowly moved toward the city of Grenoble and awaited a force under his former officer, Marshal Michel Ney, who commanded 20,000 troops under the king. Napoleon was not sure whether Ney would arrest him or join him, but when Ney and his men saw their emperor, spontaneous cheering took place. "Vive l'Empereur!"

With Ney's 20,000 men, Napoleon began to move northward toward Paris. Before he even arrived, King Louis XVIII, who was a seriously dim, disagreeable, and unpopular man, fled France after hearing that troops and men flocked to Napoleon's banner wherever he went. On March 20ᵗʰ, Napoleon entered Paris and took possession of the Tuileries Palace.

Over the next month and a half, Napoleon reformed his army. It was not the army of 1805 or even the army of 1812, but he led it, and he was joined by most of his marshals. There was also still a core of veterans to provide the recruits with some training. By June 16ᵗʰ, when he defeated the able Prussian Army at Ligny, Belgium, Bonaparte had formed an army of over 130,000 men. Napoleon knew that virtually every army in Europe would be coming for him, and he was determined to move his armies fast enough that he might defeat them one by one before they could unite.

This was not to be, as you likely know. On June 18ᵗʰ, 1815, Napoleon was defeated at Waterloo, Belgium. His marshals had committed uncharacteristic mistakes and allowed the Prussian Army to unite with a sizable English force under Wellington. Though it was close, Napoleon was beaten and forced once again to abdicate and go into exile. This time, the English were taking no chances. Napoleon's new home was the English possession of Saint Helena, an island in the South Atlantic, halfway between Brazil and Africa. There would be no escape this time.

From 1815 until he died in 1821, Napoleon lived in a small villa in Saint Helena. In actuality, he was lucky. He could easily have been executed, but his enemies did not want to make him a martyr to the French. He lived out his days in comfortable surroundings, albeit with an English guard detachment on the grounds at all times. He spent his time gardening, conversing with the daughter of the governor, and writing his memoirs.

His Legacy

The French Revolution and the Napoleonic era made a lasting impact on Europe and the Western world. The Age of Absolutism was dead or dying. In both Europe and the Americas, the ideas of the Enlightenment spread and grew. The idea of equality under the law rather than privilege by birth began to be seen as the norm, and slowly, religious freedom began to spread in Europe, though in fits and starts. Democratic ideals and political bodies rose up in places outside of England, the United States, and France. And though it would take more than a hundred years, at least in the West, women began to move toward some equality as well, winning the right to vote in the early 20th century (or regaining, as in the case of France, which had given the vote to women at the beginning of the revolution).

Napoleon's legacy has stretched throughout history. Winston Churchill kept three statues on his desk at all times: his ancestor Marlborough, who defeated Louis XIV's armies; Admiral Nelson, who defeated the French at Trafalgar; and Napoleon, whom many regard as the greatest commander in history. It has also become traditional for orchestras to play the *1812 Overture* by the Russian composer Tchaikovsky at American Fourth of July festivities. This is a bit odd, as the piece depicts Napoleon's attack on Russia and Russia's victory over him.

Illustration 41: Napoleon on the HMS Bellerophon, *depicting Napoleon on his way to exile on Saint Helena. An awed group of British officers looks on.*

Chapter 10 – The 19th Century

The First French Republic ended with the ascent of Napoleon. His empire ended with his defeat at Waterloo and exile to Saint Helena. From 1815 to 1830, France returned to the Bourbons. King Louis XVIII, who had quickly fled to avoid Napoleon's return in 1815, then returned and ruled until his death in 1824. He was followed by Charles X, the younger brother of both Louis XVI and Louis XVIII, who was then succeeded by Louis Philippe I (r. 1830–1848).

Neither Louis XVIII and Charles X were popular except among royalists, who returned to the country in droves. Both kings attempted to reinstate many of the lost privileges of both the monarchy and the nobility, though Louis XVIII was a bit more cautious out of necessity, as the revolution was still very much alive in the minds of many.

One of the major issues of the reigns of both Louis and Charles was the position of the church. Ultra-conservative Catholics in France and in Rome were eager to see ancient holdings returned to the church, but this was not going to happen. Firstly, there was too much popular support for limiting the power and influence of the church. Secondly, most of the old church lands had gone to a new rising middle class and to the Napoleonic nobility. Neither group was willing to give up such a rich prize. To attempt to do so would have united conservative middle-class businessmen with Napoleonic nobility and radical revolutionaries, who were still alive and well in Paris and other major cities, and the attempt would have resulted in utter failure.

The church was allowed to reopen seminaries and a limited number of parochial schools, but during the revolutionary and Napoleonic eras, France had built one of the first state-supported school systems in the world, and it was open to all, regardless of class, birth, or wealth.

Lastly, as had been the case with Napoleon, the bishops of France (the pope's direct representatives throughout the country) held no political power whatsoever.

Economically, France made a remarkable comeback considering the costs of the wars of the late 18th and early 19th centuries. Not only had France itself spent great treasure on these wars, but much of this treasure had belonged to other kingdoms and regions—Napoleon was as good a looter as he was a general. When the Bourbon Restoration occurred, France was made to pay a great sum to those who had finally defeated her, though it was much less than would've been expected. The European diplomats at the Congress of Vienna (also known as the Concert of Europe, meaning the nations were acting "in concert" with one another and not against each other) were determined to reestablish a conservative, balanced, and peaceful Europe after Napoleon. Welcoming France back into that circle would go some way to lessening hard feelings and resentments on all sides. Until about halfway through the century, it did, which was a remarkably long period of peace, all things considered.

French workers, both in agriculture and in France's burgeoning industries, began to enjoy greater rights and protections, though these were many times given grudgingly. Still, with these reforms, French workers slowly began to enjoy shorter hours, a six-day workweek, better pay, and, in some rare cases, compensation for injuries sustained on the job. Unemployment benefits and a social safety net would come to France before many other countries, but this did not occur until the late 19th and early 20th centuries.

The revolution that followed the French Revolution was no less important, but it did not begin in France. The Industrial Revolution, which truly began in the last quarter of the 19th century, started in Great Britain. Britain had massive coal reserves, which powered the Industrial Revolution and still powers much of our economic life today. In addition, England had iron reserves far beyond what you would think for its size. England's iron and coal reserves allowed it to rocket ahead of the other countries of Europe. Better yet, they didn't "rocket"—they "steamed ahead," for in the early part of the 19th century, steam began to power everything. Machines, ships, and the newest invention of trains were all powered by steam. Within a couple of decades, England was covered in railroads, rapidly transporting goods, raw materials, and people rapidly from place to place. One must also factor in England's worldwide empire, which supplied raw materials the English did not have and purchased finished goods. By the middle of the 19th century, England, which had a population of under twenty million people (about the population of the city of Tokyo today), dominated much of the world both economically and militarily, and it was rapidly trying to dominate the rest.

The French kings Louis XVIII and Charles X owed their thrones to England, among other countries, so they were not openly hostile to it; however, even if they wished to be, they were not equipped or prepared enough to do so. France needed a period of peace in which to reestablish herself and her power in Europe and the world. Not to say that either Louis XVIII or Charles X had any special fondness for the English. Remember, until the second decade of the 20th century, France and England had been mortal enemies for literally centuries. Old hatreds die hard.

Still, everyone recognized that peace was needed after twenty-odd years of war, so the French began their entry into the industrial world. A number of factors, a couple of which we will touch on here, kept France lagging behind other nations in Europe in terms of economic and industrial output.

Before we do that, one should be aware that the word "nation" in reference to any monarchy of Europe, no matter how small, is a misnomer, but it is an easy way for us in the 21st century to understand borders, peoples, and interests. However, aside from the United States, there really were no "nations" in the Western world at the time of the French Revolution. Oxford Languages defines the word "nation" as "a large body of people united by common descent, history, culture, or language, inhabiting a particular country or territory." Many historians, anthropologists, and sociologists might add a further definition: "A nation has also been defined as a cultural-political community that has become conscious of its autonomy, unity and particular interests."

Under the Bourbons, France was not a nation—it was the property of the king, given to him by God. The people did not feel a loyalty to the country but rather to the king, their local region, and/or a *seigneur*, or local lord. A person might think of themselves as a "subject of His Most Glorious Highness, His Excellency Louis XIV, anointed by God." But he or she might also consider themself a Norman, a Breton, or Provencal. Very rarely did these people consider themselves Frenchmen or Frenchwoman. That came with the French Revolution, and that is why the revolution is so exceedingly important—it started giving everyone a stake in the country. One of the things that Louis XVIII realized was that he was not talking to "subjects" but to "citizens." Charles X did not, and he narrowly escaped a mob bent on tearing him apart before he left the country for good in 1830.

Great Britain, which had a more liberal constitutional monarchy, was a nation, and the people of the island saw themselves that way. However, in that peculiar British way, they also saw themselves as loyal subjects of the king or queen.

The other regions of Europe, with the exception of Switzerland, were still governed by crowned heads. Some of these were more liberal than others, but all wanted to keep both their throne and their heads. They were very careful to suppress "revolutionary" ideas such as those espoused by the thinkers of the Enlightenment and the French Revolution. They succeeded or failed in varying degrees in this endeavor, with waves of revolution breaking out across the Continent once again in 1830 and again, in a more determined way, in 1848.

Although France had already experienced its revolutionary throes, the Industrial Revolution had a hard time taking root compared to England. France was a much larger country than England, and it had more large rivers, thick forests, and four mountain ranges on its borders (the Alps, Pyrenees, Vosges, and the Massif Central). This meant that the terrain of France was harder to navigate. However, France did have large quantities of wood and coal, especially in the northeast, which is where most of the French industries eventually located. By doing this, though, much of the country remained agricultural, and it depended on one small and often distant section of the nation for its industrial goods.

A couple of often overlooked factors contributed to the slowness of the French Industrial Revolution, which, despite lagging behind England, was still developing faster than many of the Italian states, eastern Europe, and Russia. The first was that, for centuries, the economic system of France meant the people were tied to the land. Peasants did not have the right to move unless it was specifically given by their *seigneur*. This meant that, in most cases, those working the land were working the same exact land that their ancestors might have. That's a strong tie. It also meant that for many, moving far from the family home was a daunting task, and many people had never been farther than a day's ride (if that) from their homes. Most of these people traveled maybe twenty miles in their entire lives.

Now, people were needed for industry, and word went out all over France. However, building and populating the factories and housing the workers was a slow process in France. Aside from the fact that many had never left their homes, there was, for many, a sort of unspoken notion that one was tied to the land. Even today, in countries from the United States to Africa, farmers find it extremely hard to leave their land and give up a long heritage and way of life.

There was also another subtle difference: religion. In the United States, many have for years been bored to tears by history professors droning on about the "Protestant work ethic" as one of the primary reasons for the United States' success. Just because it's boring doesn't mean it isn't true, though. The spread of Protestantism, beginning with the Reformation, also brought with it a change in work habits. Very generally speaking, the ideas of hard work and thrift became part of the Protestant belief system, especially among Calvinists, but one could find these ideas within all Protestant sects. Hard work and thriftiness, as opposed to sloth and luxury, which were seen as "Catholic" traits, especially among the higher-ranked bishops, were signs that one was worthy of eternal salvation. Hand in hand with this went the supplication from James 2:20 in the Bible, which is usually shortened to "Faith without works is dead," as opposed to the more Catholic idea of redemption through faith alone.

A look at the statistics of the early and middle Industrial eras will clearly show that areas that were more highly Protestant advanced faster economically during the 19th century than the Catholic areas of Europe and the United States. Of course, there were many other factors, but it definitely played an underlying role, especially in the cases of Great Britain and the United States.

If you look closely at the map below, you will notice that in areas where peasants were free to move and choose their own occupation, economic progress increased. Over the next few years, revolutions in those regions would erupt, calling for "peasant emancipation," and those areas would begin to improve economically.

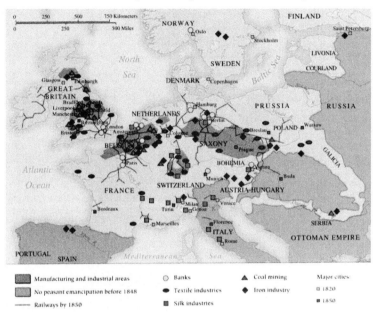

Illustration 42: You can clearly see the industrialized area of France, as well as Great Britain and Germany. These three powers would fight the world's first industrialized war beginning in 1914. (Courtesy Carnegie Learning)

1830

In the six years that Charles X ruled France, he managed to alienate nearly everyone. He attempted to restore property to *émigré* families, but the country would not support that, so he compensated them monetarily. He also always seemed to be maneuvering to bring back some form of the so-called Ancien Régime (the "Ancient Regime" of the Bourbons). The problem was, he was not a very smart man nor a good negotiator. He angered not only a large number of republican-minded people in France but also the very people he was trying to help. In addition, he was arrogant and without charm. In July 1830, he attempted to install an ultra-monarchist former prince to the position of prime minister. People saw the writing on the wall—Charles X was attempting to rule as Louis XIV had. After three days of insurrection in Paris, Charles X was chased from the city. The famous painting *Liberty Leading the People* shown earlier depicts the spirit of this event.

In Charles's place, the parliament of the people placed Louis Phillippe, a prince from a different branch of the family. He had the good fortune of being the son of the revolutionary noble Philippe Égalité, Louis XVI's cousin. Philippe Égalité voted to execute his own cousin in 1793. The three days that led to Charles X's abdication and Louis Philippe's rule are known to history as the July Days. The French people hoped that a balance might be struck between the revolutionary ideals of 1789 and the strong but controlled executive branch of the new king. The first part of Louis Philippe's reign was a relief to most Frenchmen. Yes, there were still some of the original revolutionary generation clamoring for a more radical government, but the Reign of Terror and Napoleon had made it impossible for them and their younger followers to do much other than complain.

Still, the threat of revolution kept Louis Philippe and any royalist sympathizers somewhat in check. It helped that the new king took the title "King of the French" and not "King of France"—a semantic trick that seemed to satisfy most. In his first years as king, he was actually quite popular, and he gained the nicknames of Citizen King and the Bourgeois (middle-class) King.

However, those who supported him were from both the very wealthy new middle class and the old noble families. Louis Philippe was dependent on their funds to a large degree, and as time wore on, he was pressured to move in a more conservative direction, and it seemed that he wished to move that way himself.

The changes brought about by the Industrial Revolution created new problems and confusion for both the populace and those in government. Louis Philippe and his advisers handled these problems very clumsily, and the gap between the rich and poor, which had always been wide in France, grew by leaps and bounds. This was not helped by the two years of agricultural and industrial depression. And, as we have seen, hunger is the quickest way to revolution.

In February 1848, Louis Philippe was overthrown and forced to flee to England under the name Mr. Smith. Louis Philippe named his grandson Philippe as his successor, but by this time, the French had had enough of kings. Later on, Philippe actually went to the United States for a time and fought in the US Civil War on Union General McClellan's staff. Despite other attempts by royalists to put Philippe on the throne, he never became king.

On February 26th, 1848, the National Assembly proclaimed the Second French Republic. In December of that year, a president was elected: Charles Louis Napoléon Bonaparte, the former emperor's nephew.

One of the reasons for naming Louis-Napoléon Bonaparte, who came to be known as Napoleon III, as the president was the unrest that roiled both France and much of Europe in 1848. Much like the Arab Spring of 2011, spontaneous uprisings took place in the states of Italy, the Austrian Empire, and the German states. In selecting Louis-Napoléon, the French were attempting to walk a fine line between revolutionary ideas and Napoleon's solidity and conservatism, as he was still a revered figure for many French.

Louis-Napoléon Bonaparte was not his uncle. He was not an original thinker, but he was solid, approachable, and seemed to have a wide knowledge of many subjects. Within a few months of his becoming president, things in France began to improve. They improved so much that, in 1851, after being barred legally from running for president again, he overthrew the National Assembly and proclaimed himself "President for Life." As he had in his first run for president, Louis-Napoléon used his name and his uncle's legacy as a propaganda tool, telling the French what they wanted to hear: a return to stability and glory. For the other countries of Europe, which grew alarmed at the thought of another Bonapartist army running wild over Europe, Louis promised that he would defend France but not attempt to enlarge it, at least in regards to Europe. After all, this was the beginning of the Age of Imperialism, and France, like England, was looking for new colonies in Africa and other parts of the world.

Louis-Napoléon used every power given to him by the constitution to expand his powers. He began placing men loyal to him in the administrative departments of the national and regional government apparatuses. He did the same with the army. He also successfully helped the pope regain his home in Rome after being forced from the Vatican by revolutionaries in 1848. This appealed to conservatives at home and reassured many of the other European nations, as they saw the Vatican as a stabilizing force, regardless of whether they were Protestant, Catholic, or Eastern Orthodox.

Louis's move to "President for Life" did not go unopposed, but the Republicans who fought against his regime in street battles in Paris and other major cities were outgunned and defeated. Thousands were jailed, sent to the prison camp on Devil's Island off the coast of South America, or forced overseas.

Louis-Napoléon was not completely reactionary. One of the first things he did upon becoming "President for Life" was to declare universal suffrage, allowing the vote for women to be reinstated. In November 1852, once he was secure in his position and relatively popular, Louis-Napoléon held another plebiscite. The question put to the voters was, "Should Louis-Napoléon Bonaparte be made the emperor of the French?" The results were resoundingly in favor, with 97 percent approving of the new title. Most of these votes were completely fabricated. Louis-Napoléon Bonaparte then became Napoleon III, Emperor of the French, on December 2nd, 1852.

Illustration 43: Napoleon III toward the end of his reign.

Napoleon III's rule as emperor lasted for eighteen years, seven years longer than his more famous uncle, but he remains less known. For most of his almost two decades in power, France enjoyed relative peace. There were expeditions to Mexico in an attempt to place a pro-French government in power. (Believe it or not, this is one of the main reasons why traditional Mexican music has that famous "oom-pah" band flavor. This was patterned on popular French military marches, which were about the only thing popular about the French in Mexico). France also began its colonial expansion into Africa and the Middle East during this time. Though France remained at peace with its European neighbors until the final years of Napoleon III's rule, the race for an empire brought it into fierce competition with England. This competition remained peaceful, though later in the century, this competition almost led France and England into war once again.

Under Napoleon III, France grew into Europe's largest military power once again, at least on paper and in the minds of its people and its leader. Fortunately, Louis understood that the place of France in Europe and in the world could easily be lost if he attempted to recreate his uncle's European empire.

Generally speaking, France's economy grew at a great pace throughout the Second French Empire. When Louis came to power, the nation had just over 2,000 miles of railway. When the Second French Empire fell, that number exceeded 12,000 miles, which greatly contributed to the growth of France's economy, especially in coal and steel. However, it still lagged behind Great Britain, and it would soon fall behind a new nation and powerhouse in Europe: Germany.

The Germans are an ancient people, but as a nation, Germany is ninety-five years younger than the United States. Much like ancient Gaul, the lands that comprise Germany (in all of its forms since 1870) were broken up into tribal kingdoms, which then grew into part of Charlemagne's empire and then broke up into hundreds of individual duchies, baronies, kingdoms, and bishoprics. This condition lasted until 1870, of course with many changes in borders and rulers in between.

Additionally, these different regions were often under the control or influence of foreign powers. For the most part, the states in the western part of what is now Germany were dominated by France to varying degrees. For quite some time, the smaller states in the north contended with the influence of the sometimes powerful Kingdoms of Denmark and Sweden. In the south and southeast, regions like Bavaria and others were often under Austrian sway or control.

However, beginning in the 17th century and increasing up to the time of Napoleon III, the Duchy (later Kingdom) of Prussia began its rise. This ascent was not continual, and at times, Prussia's power waned, but beginning in 1740 with the reign of Frederick II, also known as Frederick the Great (r. 1740–1786), Napoleon I's hero, Prussia became a power to be reckoned with. Initially, the growth of Prussian strength was a concern solely for the kingdoms of eastern and central Europe (Russia and Austria), but when Otto von Bismarck became the chancellor of Prussia in 1862 under King Wilhelm I (later Kaiser Wilhelm I; r.1861–1888), this new Germanic power became a direct threat to France.

The reasons are simple. First, the Prussian Army was fast becoming the best trained, best equipped, and best led in the world, though that fact remained a relative secret until 1870. Second, Otto von Bismarck was a once-in-a-generation statesman, and he knew that for the German-speaking states to become a unified nation, he would have to challenge the European powers that still held great influence over many of the German states. Specifically, these were Denmark, Austria, and France.

In 1864, Bismarck led Prussia into a war with Denmark over the succession to the Danish throne, as Bismarck wanted to have a Danish king who would be on good terms with Prussia. He also wanted to answer the question of Prussia's borders with and

Denmark, specifically the German-speaking states of Schleswig and Holstein, much of which were ruled directly by Denmark. Though no one knew the true extent of Prussian military development at the time, the outcome of the war surprised no one. The swift Prussian victory was followed by another one in 1866 against Austria, and with these moves, Prussia gained control of most of modern northern Germany, with its important ports on both the Baltic and North Seas.

In the 1864 war between Prussia and Denmark, the Prussians had been joined by the Austrians, who also had direct influence and interests in the states of Schleswig and Holstein and a number of other German states in the north near Denmark. Bismarck knew that when the war with Denmark was over, he could easily provoke a war with Austria about the power-sharing agreement the two kingdoms had reached. With increasing intensity through 1865 and the first half of 1866, the Prussians under Bismarck (with Wilhelm I's approval) began voicing "concerns" about supposed Austrian violations of their agreements. The Prussian press was tightly controlled by the government, and Bismarck, while engaging in diplomatic arguments with Austria, also stirred up Prussian popular opinion against it.

In the Seven Weeks' War of 1866, Prussia inflicted a humiliating defeat on the Austrian Empire. Until that point, Austria was thought to be one of the greatest powers of Europe, and many considered its army to be far superior to the Prussian Army in almost every way. The exact opposite was true, but even after having defeated both Denmark and Austria in two years, many in Europe, particularly France, did not understand exactly how advanced and well-trained the Prussians were.

France and Napoleon III were to realize it in 1870. Napoleon III was not his uncle, neither militarily nor politically, but he was not a stupid man. He just wasn't Bismarck, who played him like a violin. Bismarck began a series of diplomatic and political moves designed to provoke France into declaring war on Prussia. The call for war slowly built to a crescendo, starting in 1867 and continuing until July 19th, 1870, the day France finally declared war.

The diplomacy and maneuvering between France and Prussia in the run-up to the Franco-Prussian War is fascinating in and of itself, and it has filled volumes (one of which you can find at the end of this book). Suffice it to say that after about three years of provoking France in almost every way possible and making it look as if it was France and Napoleon III doing the provoking, Bismarck pulled off a diplomatic trick that left Napoleon III virtually no choice but to declare war on Prussia. If Napoleon had chosen not to do so, he might have lost his throne due to a loss of honor and influence.

In June 1870, a new king ascended to the throne of Spain. This king, Leopold, was related to the ruling house of Prussia. Napoleon III, seeing Prussian influence growing to France's east, did not want a Prussian-allied Spanish king to its south and west. After some diplomatic wrangling, Bismarck withdrew Prussian support of Leopold, which he had planned to do all along, and a new king Amadeo I, who was more acceptable to France, was put on the Spanish throne. The sticking point came when the French demanded that Prussia never again allow or put forward Leopold to be the king of Spain (at the time, Spain was an exceedingly unstable country, undergoing one coup after another since the time of Napoleon I, meaning it was likely to need a new king again). King Wilhelm, with guidance from Bismarck, refused to make this promise.

What's more, Bismarck allowed the publication of a diplomatic telegram (the Ems Telegram) describing Wilhelm's talks with French Ambassador Benedetti at the city of Ems in what is now modern-day Germany. However, the version that Bismarck sent to the Prussian newspapers, which were widely read in French diplomatic circles and newspapers, was doctored to make it seem as if Wilhelm and Benedetti had insulted each other, with the French ambassador getting the worst of it. The actual meeting was cordial, but Wilhelm refused Benedetti's demand that Prussia never back Leopold again.

Within days, French public opinion was boiling over. Combined with the growth of Prussian power on its borders and Bismarck's carefully calculated provocations over the last three years, the French and Napoleon III, who felt he needed one thing to cement his legacy—a military victory rivaling his uncle's, felt they had no choice and declared war on Prussia on July 19th.

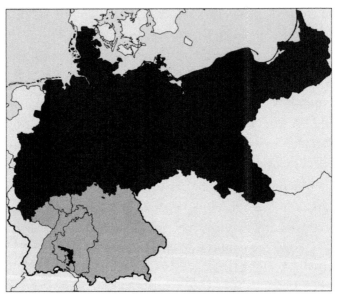

Illustration 44: Prussia and its aligned states in red, German states aligned with France (Bavaria being the largest) in gold. Alsace-Lorraine in pink.

The Franco-Prussian War lasted roughly six months and ended with a Prussian victory. In actuality, the Prussians had the war won essentially before it even began. New rapid-firing rifles and artillery, a better trained professional army with innovative tactics and strategies, and better leadership assured a Prussian victory. The key victory came at Sedan in September, after which Louis-Napoléon surrendered much but not all of his army and abdicated. The war continued until January 1871 and ended when Paris endured a siege that included much suffering and an early socialist revolution within it.

France and the world were stunned by the Prussian victory and its swiftness. The war ended all foreign influence in the German-speaking states, which now became absorbed by Prussia in the new nation of Germany with the Treaty of Frankfurt. Among the terms of the French surrender was the ceding of the provinces of Alsace and Lorraine, which included both German- and French-speaking populations, to Germany.

The fall of Napoleon III ushered in the Third French Republic, and it gave birth to a grudge that would almost cause a military dictatorship in France and a deadly rivalry with the newest and seemingly strongest European power: Germany. An entire political movement came to life in France known as "revanchism" ("revenge-ism"), and the defeat sat heavily on the hearts of Frenchmen until 1918. Léon Gambetta, a French politician who helped organize the defense of Paris, spoke for all Frenchmen about the humiliation of 1871: "Think of it always, speak of it never." The truth of this feeling among the French truly cannot be overstated.

Illustration 45: Europe after 1871. A new power in the center of the Continent, Germany, was born, and it soon challenged France, England, and Russia for dominance. (Courtesy Alex Altendorf)

Chapter 11 – The Road to WWI

The Third French Republic lasted from 1870 to 1940, when Hitler's forces marched into Paris. It was as close to the ideals of the French Revolution as any government since that tumultuous time. Since 1940, republican France has been rebuilt twice: once after WWII and another that's lasted from 1958 to this day. This means, at least as of this writing, that the Third Republic was the longest-lasting form of representative government in French history.

The Third and Fourth Republics were experiments in parliamentary rule. Though the leader of the majority party in parliament was ostensibly the leader of the country, especially in the eyes of other nations, his power was relatively weak, which was understandable after centuries of the monarchy and two emperors in less than one hundred years.

This period of stability is known, for many reasons other than its politics, as La Belle Époque, or "The Beautiful Age." It was a time when French culture rose again to lead the world, especially in the visual arts of painting and sculpture. This was the time when the names of men and women such as Monet, Manet, Degas, Gauguin, Seurat, Rodin, Toulouse-Lautrec, Mary Cassatt, and the pianist Satie became household words.

Illustration 46: Woman with a Parasol *by Claude Monet, 1875.*

Much of what people around the world revere about French culture today had its beginnings in La Belle Époque. Two of the most recognizable icons of the world, the Eiffel Tower and the Statue of Liberty, were born in this era. French food and culture spread around the Western world in the later 19th century, a time when trains and steamships brought the world closer together.

In Russia, the language of the court of the later tsars was French, and the language continued its role as the dominant one in international diplomacy, though it would be rapidly replaced by English following WWI. You may occasionally see the term "lingua franca," as in "The Swedes and the Germans use English as their lingua franca." The term seems like a misnomer, but French was so pervasive in Europe that the term, which in Latin literally means "the language of the Franks," now means a common language between people who speak two different languages.

Though French art and culture stood on their own because of their beauty and sophistication, the spread of that culture was "helped" by French participation in the second great age of European imperialism in the latter half of the 19th century.

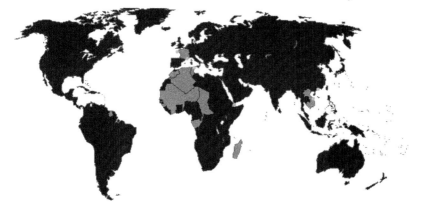

Illustration 47: The French overseas empire in 1914. The small green dots are naval coaling stations. Did you know that France retains colonies in North America? Today, it holds the two small islands of Saint-Pierre and Miquelon off the coast of Newfoundland. (Courtesy Matthew White)

As you can see from the map above, most of France's possessions were in Africa. With a few small exceptions, France dominated the African continent. Even today, many of the people of central and northwest African countries and the island of Madagascar speak a French dialect as their first or second language. In Vietnam, known then as French Indochina, much of the upper class spoke French as their primary language.

However, as you might know, much of the rest of Africa and a significant portion of the rest of the globe was ruled either directly or indirectly by Great Britain, which most people at the time recognized simply as England. The English controlled a stretch of Africa from its southern tip to Egypt. At times, as in the case of the 1898 Fashoda Incident in northeastern Africa, the English and French nearly went to war over borders, incidents, and influence.

French forces did see action when they attempted to conquer or retain control of various areas, particularly in Vietnam and Algeria.

Conflicts with Great Britain were avoided with diplomacy and common sense. The wars in Vietnam and Algeria ended with a French victory. However, there was a new problem: Germany.

In 1890, two years after the death of Kaiser Wilhelm I, his grandson, Wilhelm II, who was also the grandson of British Queen Victoria and cousins with King George V of Britain and Tsar Nicholas II of Russia, fired Bismarck, who had directed German foreign and domestic policy since 1862. In place of Bismarck's calculated, insightful, and strategic foreign policy, the Kaiser acted rashly and somewhat irrationally in what he called his desire to gain for Germany "its rightful place in the sun," meaning he wanted colonial and imperial glory for his new country.

The problem was, for the most part, two-fold. Germany was a new country, and by the time Wilhelm II was ready to embark on an imperial path, France and England, among others, had already claimed much of the world or at least the desirable parts. That left Germany to seize control of what was left in Africa, namely those areas in the central and those that were very remote and relatively poor. It also seized some islands for naval coaling stations in the Pacific. However, Wilhelm wanted more, and he felt that Britain and France were intentionally keeping it out of the race for an empire, which, to a degree, they were.

In 1905 and in 1911, Wilhelm stuck his nose into problems that France was having in North Africa, specifically Morocco. In both cases, war seemed imminent, but at the last moment, diplomacy, at times led by England, kept the two European powers from all-out war.

The Path to War

As you likely know, World War One began in 1914. Why did the most costly and deadly war in human history until that time happen?

First, for years, people (mainly in the US but elsewhere as well) believed the system of alliances set in place in the beginning part of the 20th century triggered a chain reaction due to the mutual defense clauses of these alliances.

These alliances later became the Allied Powers, which consisted of Great Britain, France, Russia, and Serbia, and it was later joined by Italy and the United States, as well as a number of smaller nations. The Central Powers were Germany, Austria-Hungary, the Ottoman Empire centered in Turkey, and Bulgaria.

The alliance system did kick in, and these nations kept their promises and declared war on their mutual enemies, but they did not have to. Yes, not doing so would cost prestige and trust, but nations had gone back on agreements since the beginning of time. So, why didn't they do so in 1914? The simple answer is the nations involved felt they had more to gain than to lose by entering the conflict.

For Great Britain, an all-powerful Germany, whose steel and coal production was already as great or slightly greater than that of the UK, with a strong navy on the Continent was too great a threat. The same was true for Russia, which shared a long border with the new power.

For France, as you can probably guess by now, the threat of Germany was three-fold. With the unity of the German states, France was no longer the most populous state in Europe. The longer war was put off (and virtually everyone knew it was coming sometime in the near future by 1898), the more the German population outgrew France. The same held true with German industrial production, which was already outpacing France. Lastly, the French saw the coalition of Great Britain, Russia, Italy, and itself as the greatest opportunity for the revenge it had been seeking since 1871.

For Germany, it believed a victorious war would, at the very least, force uneven terms from France and the likely cession of colonies from both England and France. Vast sparsely occupied lands in Russia awaited German colonization as well. This led up to what historians refer to as the Balkan powder keg. The Ottoman Empire, which had controlled much of southeast Europe for centuries, was in decline. In its place, new nations emerged or the Austro-Hungarian Empire moved in to fill the vacuum left by the Turks. The nation that concerns us most is the Kingdom of Serbia, an Eastern Orthodox nation closely aligned with Russia, which saw itself as the rightful ruler of the Southern Slavs of the Balkans, i.e., the Croats, Bosnians, Montenegrins, Slovenes, and Albanians—all of the peoples who would later make up the nation of Yugoslavia.

The problem for the Serbs was that the Austro-Hungarians, who were close allies with Germany, either directly or indirectly controlled these other Slavic lands. Though the many peoples of the area were not exactly thrilled to be under Austro-Hungarian control, they definitely did not want to be subjects of the Kingdom of Serbia. Aside from questions of religion (many South Slavs were Catholic or Muslim), the Serbs had made it no secret that as the most powerful and largest of the independent southern Slavic states, it wished to dominate the others. Under the Austro-Hungarians, the South Slavs enjoyed more autonomy than they would have under the Serbian king, Peter I.

Peter I enjoyed the life of royalty and had some say in the government, but for the most part, he was happy to let his generals and army run the country. These Serbian military men made no secret of their desire to carve out a Serbian empire in the region, and to do this, they not only built up their army but also supported underground movements within Austro-Hungarian lands where

Serbs made up a sizable minority. This was especially true in Bosnia and its capital of Sarajevo.

As you may know, on June 28th, 1914, a Serbian militant movement known as the Black Hand, which was sponsored and controlled by a Serbian officer named Dragutin Dimitrijević, aka "Apis," assassinated the Austrian heir to the throne, Archduke Franz Ferdinand, and his pregnant wife. The successful assassin, Gavrilo Princip, admitted, albeit under torture, Serbia's role in the assassination, though it was denied by the Serbs.

No one believed the denial, and within two months, most of Europe was at war. At the end of the war, Germany was blamed for starting it; however, this was not the case, though the war might likely not have occurred without it playing a role.

The Serbian king and others in the government knew about plots against the Austrians. They had been going on for years, including failed assassination attempts of the Austrian emperor, but these officials had tried to discourage the militants, knowing war with Austria was doomed to fail. However, the militants enjoyed great influence in the officer corps and much of the populace, and they could not be stopped.

However, in all honesty, the Austrians had been looking for an excuse to defeat or conquer Serbia for some time. The Serbs were a serious thorn in their side, and the assassination of Franz Ferdinand, who was not a popular figure among either his own family or the conservative army officers who wanted war, was the perfect excuse to start one. In response to the assassination, the Austro-Hungarians made demands, unreasonable ones that no nation could abide by and still retain their independence. The Serbs could not accept them, and the Austrians knew that would give them the excuse they needed to go to war.

Before they presented the Serbs with their ultimatum, the Austro-Hungarians asked their powerful ally, Kaiser Wilhelm II of Germany, whether or not he would support their actions, including going to war if Serbia's own ally, Russia, should involve itself in the conflict. Wilhelm's answer is known to history as the "blank check." He told the Austrians that he would support them no matter what. Wilhelm was keen on the opportunity to both show off his army and grab what he could from the Russians.

Though the actual timeline looks different, as it took time for news and instructions to travel, this set off the mutual defense agreements that the major nations of Europe had with each other. By August 12th, 1914, much of the European continent was at war.

You may have seen pictures or old sped-up movies of the time (you can find colorized and normal speed clips on YouTube now) showing crowds of people in various countries cheering the announcement of war and the "boys" going off to war. It's hard for us to believe now, but most people were actually happy or even elated that their nation was going to war. Today, in most cases, when nations go to war, there is perhaps a grim patriotic determination to "get things done," as there was in the United States in 2001, but not actual happiness. World War One, also known as the Great War, is what changed that mindset. After all, very few people realized what kind of a war this was going to be. Their minds still pictured war as a conflict between relatively small armies of soldiers, with civilians, for the most part, being left alone. This was not to be. World War One was the first "industrialized war," and the new weapons that had been developed in the years before and during it would turn the fields of Europe and elsewhere (for instance, in Africa, where major combat took place between the Germans and English) into graveyards.

The French went into WWI believing their army was the best in Europe. They had used the years between 1871 and 1914 to modernize and retrain their men, and they could call up millions of military-aged men to serve. Their factories turned out immense numbers of shells, bullets, and guns, as did Great Britain's and Germany's.

This is not a book on military history, so the major battles will not be examined in any depth. In this chapter, we will provide you with the important facts and the results of WWI from a French perspective.

Before we get into the war, it should be said, especially for some of our American readers who might have a bias against the French military in World Wars I and II, that among the Allied Powers, the French only lost fewer men than the Russians and slightly fewer than the Germans. However, it must be remembered that the Russians were covering a greater area and had more men to begin with and that the Germans were fighting on two fronts. French deaths in WWI numbered nearly 1.4 million. Great Britain's losses, which includes Ireland, amounted to 750,000. Of course, this is still a staggering number and represents a large portion of its military-aged population. For the most part, the French poilus (the French term for their soldiers at the time, meaning "hairy ones" for their ubiquitous beards and mustaches) fought with incredible bravery and tenacity. At the Battle of Verdun in 1916 alone, the French sustained 400,000 casualties. The number of French dead at that one battle was roughly equal to the 117,000 US dead in the eight months that the Americans took part in the combat. The Battle of Verdun brought about the slogan that motivated the French to victory in the battle and the war: "On ne passe pas!" "They shall not pass!"

Illustration 48: "On ne passe pas!" by Maurice Neumont, 1918.

Well, at least the *Boche* (the pejorative French name for the German soldier, meaning "string bean," named after the color of their uniforms) didn't make it to Paris or win at Verdun. But in 1914, and again in the spring of 1918, the Germans came close.

In 1914, the French rallied along the Marne River not far from Paris and stopped the Germans after a bloody battle. In 1918, the Germans were able to transfer hundreds of thousands of men from Russia, who had dropped out of the war after the Bolsheviks of Vladimir Lenin came to power, to the Western Front for one last push before the Americans were able to bring their full strength to bear. The Americans entered the war in late 1917. In their famous Spring Offensive of 1918, the Germans, using innovative tactics and fresh men, almost broke through French, British, and American lines to Paris, but they were stopped. After this last offensive, the Germans were no longer able to continue in any meaningful way. Like most wars, WWI was fought using the tactics and methods of the previous war, at least until its very last days. You likely have seen movies, documentaries, or pictures of troops from all nations going over the top of the trenches that covered the Western Front from the border of Switzerland to the English Channel. You probably also know that in many cases, the order to go "over the top" was a death sentence. This was because, by the outbreak of the war, weapons had changed.

Even though the French had experienced the German innovations of the rapid-firing rifle and artillery in the Franco-Prussian War of 1870–71 and then adopted them themselves, many believed the outcome was sort of a fluke, the product of bad planning and leadership. Surely, older French generals, who had grown up on stories of Napoleon I and had even known veterans of the Napoleonic Wars, said to themselves that a hard-driven attack led by able officers and driven home at the right time and place would win the day.

The vast majority of generals and politicians in the combatant nations recognized the need for the use of newer weapons, primarily the machine gun and, as the war went on, the airplane, poison gas, the flame thrower, the tank, and faster-firing, longer-ranged, and deadly artillery. However, these men did not seem to recognize how much these weapons changed warfare. Men charged over the top into fields pocked with shell holes only to be cut down like wheat at harvest.

Making things even worse was that, in the time between 1870 and 1914, industrialization had vastly improved guns, cannons, bullets, and shells, and they were being turned out and used at an unbelievable rate. To name just one country, Germany estimated it had fired over 220,000,000 artillery shells during the war. Most of these were fired in the concentrated areas of the Western Front. Artillery barrages sometimes lasted for days without end. Men went permanently insane. Many developed such incredible shell shock (the WWI-term for PTSD) that they could no longer control their bodies, in the worst cases developing Parkinson-like tremors and outright shaking. No one knows exactly how many of the casualties of the artillery bombardments during WWI were actually suicides, men taking their own lives rather than endure more shelling.

All of this led to serious problems in morale, and the French experienced it on a greater level than the other nations, though all certainly suffered from it. In 1917, mass mutinies gripped the French Army. Had the extent of these mutinies been known, some historians believe the Germans may likely have been able to win the war or at least gain Paris.

All along the line, French soldiers simply refused to fight. Some dropped their guns and walked off. Most were arrested. Many left for home. Others kept their weapons and threatened officers who ordered them "over the top." Most of the mutineers declared they would willingly defend their ground but not attack. At the time, many French politicians believed the poilus to be under the influence of a small number of socialist or communist revolutionaries, as had happened in Russia, but this really wasn't the case. Most of the mutineers—and there were thousands of them—were patriotic men who had already been asked to sacrifice a lot. They were willing to sacrifice even more but not for poor leaders who cared nothing for them. Plenty of French generals were like that, primarily the supreme commander, General Robert Nivelle, who had promised a quick victory when the French began the Second Battle of the Aisne in April 1917. Needless to say, the victory did not occur, and scores upon scores of poilus were cut down. This was when the mass mutinies began.

Though public belief is that hundreds of soldiers were arrested and brought before firing squads, the truth was that under Nivelle and then his successor, Philippe Pétain (a hero in WWI, a traitor in WWII), only about one hundred executions took place, though it's likely that not all were documented. Between the executions and reforms that took place as a result of the mutinies and changes in command, the mutinies ended. Morale was also helped by the election of the new prime minister of France, Georges Clemenceau, who promised additional reforms in the army as well as victory.

Illustration 49: Colorized photo of battle-hardened French soldiers on guard duty in Paris toward the end of the war. Resting on their rifles is their battle-scarred unit banner.

By the fall of 1918, the Germans and Austrians were on their last legs. The German Spring Offensive had failed, and the Austrians were taking massive casualties in Pyrrhic victories against Italy in the Alps. In both the German and Austrian armies, soldiers began to mutiny as the French had in 1917. The leadership of the German Army knew that they could not hope to hold back the Allies on the Western Front much longer. They realized that to prevent the Allies from marching into Germany itself, terms for peace should be sought.

Let's be clear. In the fall of 1918, the German government was being run by two generals, Erich Ludendorff and Paul von Hindenburg. They, along with the vast majority of their fellow commanders, believed that continuing the war was useless. By the beginning of November, Kaiser Wilhelm II was a shell of himself (and he was not a stable person to begin with), and he was under great pressure to abdicate in favor of a civilian government headed by the popular Social Democrats. Strikes, demonstrations, and mutinies were rife in Germany and its armed forces.

Wilhelm essentially ceded power to the Social Democrats by the beginning of November 1918. They, as well as the army high command, knew the war had to end. However, in a shrewd political move, the generals declared that they would not approach the Allies for peace, for that was the government's job. And with that, one of the largest and costliest lies in the history of mankind was born, for, in November of 1918, the politicians of Germany were still behind the army, which was in power both on the front and at home. The next chapter, which touches on the lead-up to the next world war, will discuss this further.

At the beginning of November, the German government sent out peace feelers to the Americans, not the French or the British. The French would likely have rejected them out of hand, while the British were on the fence. The populations of both nations had large numbers of people pushing for the complete defeat and conquest of Germany after all the bloodshed. The US president, Woodrow Wilson, had put forward what is known as his Fourteen Points for peace. In Germany's eyes, the growing power and influence of America made it seem like the best path toward a ceasefire. After that, a permanent peace could then be negotiated. This is what occurred, and on November 11th, 1918, World War I came to an end.

Chapter 12 – Versailles and between the Wars

The Captivating History series includes an excellent book on the Treaty of Versailles, which ended WWI, as well as detailed books on both world wars. What follows here is a brief summary of the fateful Treaty of Versailles.

The Paris Peace Conference, whose members would hammer out a permanent peace to WWI, began in mid-January 1918. France was represented by its prime minister, Georges Clemenceau, a veteran politician and journalist. He was nicknamed "the Tiger" for his fierceness in defending the causes in which he believed. In January 1919, that cause was punishing Germany, the nation that had humiliated France when Clemenceau was a young man and that had inflicted over a million deaths on the battlefield and hundreds of millions of dollars in economic damages in its four-year occupation of Flanders and the western border regions, which were France's richest and most developed industrial areas.

Emotionally and psychologically, Clemenceau and the French were also keen to punish Germany for taking Alsace-Lorraine after the French defeat in 1871. Politically, Clemenceau also knew that his continued place as the head of the French government depended on taking a strong stand against the Germans, for most Frenchmen and women were eager to punish Germany for wrongs both real and imagined.

Joining Clemenceau as the main players at the Paris Conference were British Prime Minister David Lloyd George, Italian Prime Minister Vittorio Orlando, and US President Woodrow Wilson.

Wilson had established himself as a power player at the talks with his arrival in France just a few weeks before. Greeted as a savior and representative of the nation that many viewed as the guarantor of victory in WWI and the best hope for a lasting peace, Woodrow Wilson enjoyed Beatles-like popularity when he arrived in France. He was literally mobbed everywhere he went. Streets and boulevards throughout France were named after him and his country. For instance, in beautiful Mediterranean Nice, two of the main streets of the city are Avenue Woodrow Wilson and Avenue des États-Unis ("Avenue of the United States").

Wilson had formulated (actually, most of the formulation was done by aides) his now-famous Fourteen Points, which were a set of guidelines for nations to follow in the future. Wilson, who viewed these guidelines more as rules, believed that once nations adopted his principles, war could be averted forever. Of these points (found in Appendix A at the end of this book in simplified form), Points 1, 2, 3, and 14 were the foundation stones of Wilson's permanent peace plan. Point 14, which led to the foundation of the League of Nations, the forerunner of today's United Nations, was the most important to the US president; he was willing to bargain away other points if he could achieve the creation of such a league. (Ironically, because of Wilson's arrogant personality and domestic American politics, the United States Senate refused to ratify the Treaty of Versailles and join the League of Nations.)

Vittorio Orlando of Italy was essentially sidelined. Italy was viewed as not having a right to the same voice as the other major powers and was essentially given table scraps in its post-war desires.

Lloyd George and the British were split on how the Germans should be treated. They, like the French, had expended much blood in the war. Great Britain, which was the richest nation on Earth before the war, had gone broke by 1916 and relied on US loans to keep afloat, as did the French. Many in the United Kingdom wished the same type of revenge as the French did, but many, including Lloyd George, had misgivings about treating Germany too harshly.

Aside from the return of Alsace-Lorraine to France, both Great Britain and the French demanded reparations from the Germans. Diplomatically, reparations are monetary penalties for the damages caused by war. The French demanded an exorbitant amount. The British argued among themselves and finally settled on an amount less than the French had demanded and more than the Americans had proposed.

Both the British and Americans were concerned that if exorbitant reparation payments were demanded, Germany, which was an economic powerhouse before the war, might never recover. This would affect their trade and the economies of the other European nations, which could possibly throw the world into a depression. The French did not care. They wanted payback.

In their minds, they were entitled to it, and objectively, they were. Many people criticize the Treaty of Versailles for its treatment of Germany and the part it played in the rise of Adolf Hitler, but Versailles was comparatively mild compared to the Treaty of Brest-Litovsk and what it demanded of the Soviet Union (what Russia became after 1917) when Lenin sued for peace. In that treaty, the Soviets were forced to give up nearly 20 percent of its land and millions upon millions of dollars in reparations, among other things. Thus, German complaints about Versailles fell on deaf French ears.

Perhaps what rankled the Germans the most was a clause put into the treaty that is known as the "War Guilt Clause." This meant that Germany bore responsibility for starting the war, which it clearly did not. However, since the end of the war, both the Ottoman and Austro-Hungarian Empires ceased to exist, instead consisting of small, poor rump states that had no money or influence. Germany was the only Central Power left, and it had never been invaded or even shelled. German industry was intact. The Germans had also "signed" the "Blank Check" to Austria, which allowed the war to accelerate and spread. During the war, the Germans had invaded neutral Belgium and conducted a harsh and atrocity-laden occupation. In the eyes of the French and British, as well as many Americans, Germany started the war.

The Treaty of Versailles laid down the outlines of the peace. A dozen or so ancillary treaties listed the details. In the end, the Germans had no choice. Their army was in shambles. They were facing communist revolutions in parts of the homeland. Their economy was a mess. The WWI chapter needed to be closed so Germany could move on, or so the thinking went. The Social Democrat politicians and diplomats representing Germany in Paris signed the treaty. And from that moment on, the German armed forces and new right-wing extremist parties (the Nazis were but one of many) would blame the Social Democrats for signing away Germany's "honor," its economy, its army, and more. The men that Hindenburg and Ludendorff put forward to sign the treaty were known by many in Germany as the "November Criminals," named for the month in which the hostilities ended. Among the people calling them that were Paul von Hindenburg, Erich Ludendorff, and an Austrian-born German Army veteran named Adolf Hitler.

Illustration 50: William Orpen's The Signing of the Treaty of Versailles in the Hall of Mirrors. *Seated at center left with the mustache is Georges Clemenceau. Dead center is David Lloyd George. To the left of Clemenceau is Wilson, then Orlando of Italy.*

Chapter 13 – WWII

For France, the Second World War, at least in terms of human life, was less costly than the first. And while the First World War most certainly left a lingering psychological, emotional, and political legacy as we will soon see, it is perhaps the disaster and division of WWII that left a greater impact.

Though the German invasion of France in 1940 was absolutely an unmitigated disaster for France, it should be remembered that about half of the approximately 220,000 French military deaths that took place in WWII took place in that short period. Today, many people in Great Britain and the United States falsely believe that the French simply laid down their guns after the first few shots were fired and raised the white flag of surrender. Yes, there is a marked contrast between the performance of the French military in World War I and the beginning years of World War II, but to overlook those deaths is wrong. By comparison, the United States fought for about ten years in Vietnam. The total killed in action was just under 60,000 men. This does not diminish the sacrifice of those men but illustrates the great bloodshed that took place.

Toward the end of the German invasion, Prime Minister Winston Churchill of Great Britain, dismayed by the reports he was getting about the lack of French resistance and the beginnings of large-scale surrenders, asked, "Why don't they fight?" Of course, Churchill was, well, Churchill, and he likely would've fought until the Germans had invaded his own home. However, his view was tainted by the experience of WWI. In the First World War, Churchill had been Britain's first lord of the admiralty, and he resigned in disgrace over a battle in which he played a large part. After that, he voluntarily fought on the frontlines of the Western Front for six months, where he admired the French soldiers and officers he met and saw before he returned to England to serve as the minister of munitions for the remainder of the war.

World War I was not World War II. To put it simply, the difference lay in how Germany fought. The Germans utilized the new technologies that had been developed during and after WWI, and they had much better field commanders and a better plan than the French did. At the end of the First World War, France had a huge standing army and occupied small parts of western Germany, which it would continue to do to varying degrees until 1922 and again from 1923 to 1925 after it felt Germany had reneged on parts of the peace treaty. However, like most nations after a prolonged conflict, the French people and its soldiers wanted normalcy, and demobilization began on a large scale.

As the 1920s merged into the Great Depression of the 1930s and people all over the world became more concerned with surviving, they became less and less concerned about what was happening in other countries. Within France, political extremes grew, just as they did elsewhere. On the left, communists and socialists (from the more radical to the moderate) saw that the sacrifices of WWI seemed to have meant nothing: the rich were still rich and growing richer. The poor, and now much of the middle class, was growing poorer. Germany was a rising power again by this point, and it seemed to many on the left in all nations that the "conservative powers that be" were more interested in using Hitler to contain the Soviet Union and socialism of all kinds than they were in improving the lives of the people. In Britain, as well as France, people asked, "Is this why we fought the war?"

In France, those on the right wing both admired and feared Hitler. The French political right, like its left, was splintered into many factions and viewpoints, but as the 1930s went on and fascism spread from Italy (1922) to Germany (1932–33) and then to Spain (1936), more French conservatives became fascist in outlook themselves. Before the war, this meant that while they admired Hitler's government and many of its principles (including violent anti-Semitism), they were all in favor of a strong and assertive French military and foreign policy to both compete with and counter Germany and, to a lesser degree, Italy.

Of course, most people inside France in the 1930s were moderate in their political views, but generally speaking, politics usually finds a balance, and unless threatened directly, moderates tend to remain silent. Unfortunately, in the 1930s, things in France continued to get worse, not better, and the ranks of those on both ends of the political spectrum grew while those in the middle began to feel helpless in the face of both domestic and foreign events.

In a way, France was at war with itself before the outbreak of WWII. The 1920s saw great changes around the world and in France. Internationally, France saw its influence wane as the power of the United States grew. Economically, politically, and culturally, America was becoming a superpower, and within France, many either welcomed the change coming from across the ocean or resented it.

Economically and politically, France was still a world power, but it was clear to almost everyone (at least outside France) that she was in decline, at least in comparison to the United States. In reality, not much could be done about that.

Culturally, changes coming from the United States came in the form of music, literature, and the arts, including the new medium of film. Charlie Chaplin was as popular in France as he was in the United States (of course, Chaplin was British, but his films were made in Hollywood). American influence also began to be felt in the world of fashion, which had long been dominated by France. While many, especially among the young and urban populations, embraced these changes and trends, many older French people and those living in smaller towns and the country saw these changes as symptomatic of French decline, and they looked for someone to blame. They blamed the left, while those on the left began to view the right as backward, chauvinistic (both in terms of the role of women and nationalistically), racist, and out of touch.

Interestingly, many black American jazz musicians, like Josephine Baker and Louis Armstrong, made a second home in France. There were two reasons for this. The urban French loved jazz, and, for the most part, at least in the cities, the French were much more racially tolerant than most Americans.

However, France also had an ugly side. While many accepted black Americans, they were a sort of novelty. The French retained their colonial empire after WWI and even expanded it into the Middle East, which meant that growing numbers of immigrants from Asia, the Middle East, and especially Africa came to France for economic gain. This spurred a backlash among many in France, and even highly educated and French-speaking men, such as the future leader of North Vietnam, Ho Chi Minh, could only find menial jobs as dishwashers and the like.

On the right, many French believed that France should be for the French, not outsiders. And increasingly, those outsiders came to include French and other European Jews, many of whom had lived in France for centuries. It's an axiom that when times get bad economically or otherwise, scapegoats are looked for, and in

Europe, ever since the fall of the Roman Empire, that meant blaming the Jews.

Anti-Semitism has a long and ugly history in both France and the world. There are clear historical reasons for it—not that those reasons are justified or acceptable; they are not. That story is too long for this book, but suffice it to say that while France, generally speaking, was more accepting of its Jewish countrymen than most other nations in Europe, especially those in the east, anti-Semitism still existed.

This was made clear in the famous Dreyfus affair in the late 19th century. Briefly, French military officer Alfred Dreyfus, who was Jewish, was accused of passing French military secrets to the Germans. Dreyfus was convicted on the flimsiest of evidence (he was later exonerated) and sentenced to life in prison on the notorious Devil's Island prison off the coast of South America. The trial, which took place in the late 1890s, captivated and consumed France from top to bottom, famously including the writer Émile Zola, who came to the defense of Dreyfus and had to flee the country because of it.

When Dreyfus was convicted, he was paraded publicly in Paris, where he was stripped of his insignia and disgraced. The crowd began to chant anti-Semitic slurs and almost got out of control. Though it was later shown that another officer had betrayed his country, the Dreyfus affair exposed the deep anti-Semitism within France, which many believed was not there. When the Germans occupied France, that latent anti-Semitic feeling came to the fore.

One last thing about pre-war France. In France, as in many other countries, the Great Depression showed the vast differences between the rich and poor. Additionally, France had become an industrial power, and millions of people worked in factories throughout the country, though agriculture still played a huge role in the life of the nation (as it does today). Throughout the 1920s and especially in the 1930s, strikes and other protests took place in an attempt to improve the economic lives of the workers. At times, these strikes and demonstrations were put down violently, oftentimes including fatalities.

Those not involved directly either supported the strikers in their desire for a better life or condemned them for making a bad situation worse. In the eyes of many in France, both moderates and conservatives, many of the strikers were self-proclaimed socialists or, even worse, communists following the line put out by Moscow, home of the Comintern, or Communist International. These strikes helped the workers on some occasions, but they also brought down governments and further divided France.

The Maginot Line

In the 1920s, military thinking underwent a series of revolutions. The advent of the airplane, especially the long-range bomber, the submarine, and, perhaps most significantly for France, the tank changed the way military men thought about war. However, one revolution took hold within much of the French military, that of static fortification.

Hoping to avoid a repeat of the carnage of men going over the top of trenches, French generals, especially its minister of war in the late 1920s and first two years of the 1930s, André Maginot, began to find a way to defend France. They wanted to prevent another German invasion, major French casualties in future wars, and the need for a large standing peacetime army, as going without one would allow more men to contribute to the economy. The result was the famous (or infamous) Maginot Line, which was constructed at a great cost between 1930 and 1939.

The Maginot Line was a modern wonder, running some 280 miles from the Swiss border to the Belgian border with France (though, with its twists and turns, it ran a total of 900 miles). Massive walls, cannons, machine guns, bunkers, tunnels, headquarters, canteens, and small underground factories were contained in the line. It was virtually impregnable to frontal assault.

Illustration 51: Retractable cannons and machine gun turrets of the Maginot Line today.

The problem with the Maginot Line was three-fold. First, it gave the French a defensive mindset, so when the time for offensive action came, many French officers were ill-prepared. Second and most importantly, the line did not stretch to cover France's border with Belgium in any meaningful way, which means the Germans could simply drive around its main fortifications to the south. Third, when the Maginot Line was outflanked in 1940, French military and civilian morale plummeted, which makes sense, as they had been told that they were safe behind its fortifications for years. This was made even worse when it was realized that for all the money and resources spent on the line, over five thousand additional tanks and five battleships could have been built.

The French only began to build fortifications along the Franco-Belgian border in the last two years before the war when it received signals from the Belgians that they might once again declare neutrality in any coming war (not that it had saved them in WWI) or might choose to not fight against an overpowering Germany. By the time actual combat broke out in 1940, the Maginot Line along the Belgian border was porous, with huge gaps between installations, many of which were only partially complete.

Why didn't the French build the Maginot Line along the Belgian border to begin with? One, it was thought that building the line there might indicate to the Belgians that the French would not fight for them in the coming conflict. Two, French and British military doctrine called for Allied troops to move forward into Belgium to prevent a repeat of WWI. Three, it was costly—immensely costly—and the Great Depression was still taking place.

The War

On September 1st, 1939, Germany invaded Poland, and the British and French, having signed a mutual defense pact with the Poles, declared war on Germany on September 3rd. Everyone in France and Britain prepared for immediate conflict. It did not come. From September 1939 to May 1940, the two sides fought what many sarcastically called the Phony War. Yes, there had been combat in Norway when the Germans invaded that country in April 1940, but that was far away and relatively inconsequential, at least to most Frenchmen.

Additionally, the French had launched a minor offensive into the German Saar region, penetrating about six miles without much resistance. They went no farther for reasons that still baffle historians, but with no real German reaction, many in France believed the Nazis were afraid of attacking France again.

Of course, we know this was one of the grossest misjudgments in history. The Germans had precise plans for their invasion of France, and on May 10th, the Germans unleashed the "Blitzkrieg ("lightning war") against France, Belgium, and Holland. British and French troops rushed into Belgium as agreed. The bulk of the French Army waited for the main German invasion along the Maginot Line.

The Germans did invade Belgium, and slowly (then rapidly, after events occurred in the south), they pushed back the British Expeditionary Force (BEF) and the French. Along the Maginot Line, the Germans allowed the French to see and hear what they thought was the bulk of the German Army. The Germans shelled, bombed, and launched local attacks along the strongest part of the Maginot Line to hold the French in place and to fool them into thinking the main attack would come there.

Meanwhile, on the borders of France, Belgium, and Luxembourg, in the "impassable" (or so it was thought) Ardennes Forest, the bulk of the Germans' tanks moved forward undetected. The Maginot Line did not cover the area of the Ardennes. And why would it? The forest was too thick and the roads too bad for a large force, especially an armored one. This means the Germans attacked the French at the perfect place: between their mobile army in Belgium and the static Maginot Line. Within days, the Germans had penetrated deep behind French lines and were moving toward the English Channel to cut off the BEF and French forces in Belgium and to move behind the Maginot Line in the south.

What many people don't know is that the French had more and better tanks than the Germans. What they didn't have were better officers, better trained men, a fighting spirit, and a better plan.

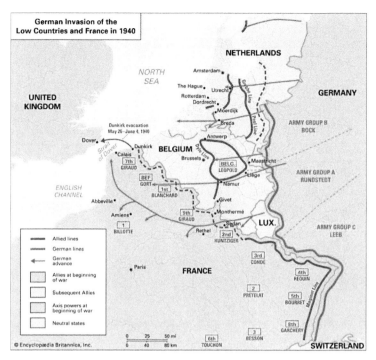

Illustration 52: The Western Front from
May to June 1940. (Courtesy Brittanica.com)

In the years prior to the war, the French High Command had allowed itself to believe that the Maginot Line would be effective and that the next war would be fought as the last had. Obviously, they were wrong on both counts. They would have been better off listening to maverick officers, most notably an officer named Charles de Gaulle, as they had independently developed and studied other ideas of mobile warfare in what would prove to be the "Age of the Tank." These officers, like the vast majority of their German counterparts and a handful of British officers, believed that the use of massed armor against an enemy's weak point, in combination with strong air and artillery attacks at the point of assault, was how future wars would be fought. French, British, and American tank doctrine placed small groups of tanks within infantry units as support units and not as the main weapon of war. As you can see from the map on the previous page, the Germans cut off the bulk of the French and British forces, which resulted in the BEF's evacuation at Dunkirk and the mass surrender of much of the French Army. It should be remembered, however, that two important things happened in that evacuation. A large number of French soldiers went into exile in England and formed the core of the Free French Forces, and that, given the right motivation, the French could fight. One reason the British were able to evacuate so many men, in addition to their own tenacity, air cover, and still supreme navy, was the tenacity of the French in holding the Germans back. The French under de Gaulle had also put modern tank warfare into action in a counteroffensive at Arras, temporarily halting the Germans there.

On June 22nd, 1940, the French officially surrendered to Hitler at Compiègne in the same train car they had used to dictate the terms of the ceasefire of WWI. When the ceremonies were finished, Hitler had the train car blown up.

Prior to that, on June 14th, German troops did what had previously been thought impossible: they marched down the Champs-Élysées in Paris. The famous picture below, taken from a film clip, captures the feeling of most Frenchmen and women at the time.

All was not completely lost for France, however. With an invasion of England already in mind and other future plans, including a war on the Soviet Union, Hitler allowed the French to govern themselves in a semi-autonomous area known as Vichy France, named for its capital at the southern city of Vichy.

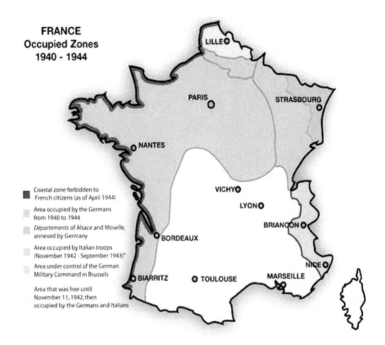

FRANCE
Occupied Zones
1940 - 1944

LILLE

PARIS

STRASBOURG

NANTES

Coastal zone forbidden to
French citizens (as of April 1944)

Area occupied by the Germans
from 1940 to 1944

Départements of Alsace and Moselle,
annexed by Germany

Area occupied by Italian troops
(November 1942 - September 1943)"

Area under control of the German
Military Command in Brussels

Area that was free until
November 11, 1942, then
occupied by the Germans and Italians

VICHY

LYON

BRIANÇON

BORDEAUX

NICE

BIARRITZ   TOULOUSE   MARSEILLE

In charge of the Vichy government was the hero of WWI, Marshal Philippe Pétain. In the years since the first war, Pétain and the men loyal to him had become increasingly conservative to the point of being fascist. Many of them looked to Hitler as a role model, and when given the opportunity, they wasted no time in implementing fascist policies in Vichy.

At first, this did not include the same kind of persecution Jews were facing in other parts of the Nazi empire, despite pressure from the Germans. However, as time went on, more and more anti-Semitic policies were enacted. Still, many Jews from occupied France fled into Vichy, as it was a place of relative safety when the Germans began rounding up Jewish people in the occupied parts of France in the late summer of 1941.

The history of the Holocaust in France takes up thousands upon thousands of pages. Comparatively speaking, fewer Jews (as a percentage of the pre-war population of some 400,000) were killed than in other European countries. A great deal of this was due to the brave French people who helped to evacuate large numbers of

Jews to Britain, Spain, and Portugal, as well as others who helped to hide them from their persecutors. In all, about 75,000 French Jews perished in the camps of the about 400,000 living in France before the war.

Though the French may have averted the kind of horror that took place in Poland and the USSR, the Nazi occupation of the country and its puppet state in Vichy, which ceased to exist as a "state" in late 1942 due to German fears of an invasion there, illustrated that many French, like many people in other countries, would turn a blind eye to or, worse, take part in the persecution of an entire people based on their birth.

This brings us to those who did not turn a blind eye or join the fascists: the famed French Resistance.

The Resistance began almost as soon as the combat ended. At first, resistance meant slowing down work, not being pleasant to the Germans, and providing safe shelter to French soldiers, who were required to report to the Germans before returning home or heading to prisoner of war camps, among other "smaller" actions.

Most Frenchmen, however, preferred to see which way the wind blew, and in 1940/41, it was blowing from Germany. At the time, Germany seemed invincible, and many people came to terms with that. Some welcomed the Germans, while others tolerated them. Most did not resist. Even to the end of the war, those active in the Resistance was a small percentage of the population, though it grew to sizable numbers by 1944. Estimates range from 100,000 to close to 500,000 men and women, the latter playing an exceedingly important role as agents, saboteurs, and in leadership.

The face of the Resistance ultimately became that of Charles de Gaulle, who left France and immediately began organizing a government in exile, an army, and a resistance movement. De Gaulle is both loved and hated within France and without to this day, but no matter how one feels about him, it cannot be denied that Charles de Gaulle (who was seriously wounded multiple times, captured, and organized escape attempts in WWI) was brave, cunning, supremely confident, and above all, patriotic. On June 18th, 1940, he made what is known to history as the Appeal of 18 June from England:

The leaders who, for many years, were at the head of French armies, have formed a government. This government, alleging our armies to be undone, agreed with the enemy to stop fighting. Of course, we were subdued by the mechanical, ground and air forces of the enemy. Infinitely more than their number, it was the tanks, the airplanes, the tactics of the Germans which made us retreat. It was the tanks, the airplanes, the tactics of the Germans that surprised our leaders to the point to bring them there where they are today. But has the last word been said? Must hope disappear? Is defeat final? No! Believe me, I speak to you with full knowledge of the facts and tell you that nothing is lost for France. The same means that overcame us can bring us to a day of victory. For France is not alone! She is not alone! She is not alone! She has a vast Empire behind her. She can align with the British Empire that holds the sea and continues the fight. She can, like England, use without limit the immense industry of United States. This war is not limited to the unfortunate territory of our country. This war is not finished by the battle of France. This war is a world wide war. All the faults, all the delays, all the suffering, do not prevent there to be, in the world, all the necessary means to one day crush our enemies. Vanquished today by mechanical force, we will be able to overcome in the future by a superior mechanical force. The destiny of the world is here. I, General de Gaulle, currently in London, invite the officers and the French soldiers who are located in British territory or who would come there, with their weapons or without their weapons, I invite the engineers and the special workers of armament industries who are located in British territory or who would come there, to put themselves in contact with me.

Whatever happens, the flame of the French resistance must not be extinguished and will not be extinguished.

Most people did not hear the speech, especially in France, but his words, along with another more widely heard speech on June 22nd, spread by print throughout the country and helped keep alive and spark the spirit of resistance in France.

The Resistance was not one movement. Not all Resistance fighters listened to de Gaulle. Some were led by other officers. Some of the most active Resistance cells were run and manned by communists taking orders from Moscow. Others were just individuals acting according to their conscience, but as the war went on and as the British and Americans began to recognize de Gaulle as the leader of France in exile, more and more people and groups gelled around de Gaulle, at least loosely.

Resistance acts took many shapes. Much of it was reconnaissance, reporting on German activities of all kinds, whether it be economic, military, or political. Some were acts of sabotage, and there were some assassinations. Much of the Resistance was in the form of disseminating information, such as underground newspapers, leaflets, and graffiti. By doing this, Resistance fighters let the French know there was a resistance movement all around them, that they were not alone, and not to collaborate with the Germans. Since much of the Resistance's activity was against its fellow Frenchmen cooperating with the Germans, things became extremely violent, and in essence, there was a French civil war within WWII.

Illustration 53: The Appeal of 18 June above a memorial to a Resistance fighter: "In this house lived Alexandre ROCHAIS born on 3 August 1886 a fighter of the 6th section of ARAC, arrested 9 June 1943, assassinated 18 September 1943 at Buchenwald." These signs are ubiquitous in France.

Though there were many heroes of the Resistance (and one can see signs on buildings throughout France honoring their sacrifice, like the one above), one man, besides de Gaulle, has become the face of the Resistance: Jean Moulin, a man of extraordinary bravery.

Jean Moulin was a civil servant, a regional governor or "prefect," before the war. When the Nazis took over, he was almost immediately arrested and tortured for defending French African colonial troops against false charges of rape. He was released when he refused to bend and used a shard of broken glass to cut his own throat, almost taking his life in the process.

Upon his release, he sought out other like-minded people and joined the Resistance. He soon came to the attention of de Gaulle as someone who knew many within France and who was an organizer and a patriot. Over the course of the next two and half years, Moulin, aka "Rex," served as de Gaulle's eyes and ears in France, many times just escaping capture. Sadly, though, he was betrayed from within by a collaborator, and he was taken by the Germans, tortured, and sent to Germany on a train, where he arrived dead. Today, his remains are honored in the Pantheon in Paris, a monument and memorial to the great Frenchmen and women of history.

Illustration 54: Modern French stamp honoring Jean Moulin.

For almost every major act of resistance, the Germans punished the population as a way to turn the rest of France against those who were resisting, which was a tactic they used everywhere. For every German soldier killed or attacked, hostages were taken and, many times, executed. In 1944, as the Germans were attempting to send troops from southern France to attack the Allied landing in Normandy, one of their most notorious units, the 2nd SS Armored Division "Das Reich" was bombed incessantly by Allied planes and harassed by Resistance units. In response to a report that a German officer had been killed in the area, one company of *Das Reich* went berserk, wiping out the nearby village of Oradour-sur-Glane in central France. This included the deaths of civilians locked in a burning church. Six hundred people, including 247 children, were killed. Today, Oradour stands *exactly* as it was on the day following the massacre, a silent memorial to those who fell during yet another tragic moment of the war.

Illustration 55: Oradour-sur-Glane, France.

Outside of France, de Gaulle's Free French grew slowly with Allied help and a regular infusion of escapees from the Continent. In 1942, they proved their worth in a brave battle at Bir Hakeim in Libya. Though it was a military defeat, the outnumbered French at Bir Hakeim held off a much larger German force for a month. The German officer in command said after the war that he had not fought a superior opponent throughout the entire war.

In 1944, Free French commandos and air and naval forces took part in the D-Day landings, and later that summer, they aided in the invasion of southern France, which was named Operation Dragoon. As part of both of these landings, Resistance fighters, many times joined by Allied agents and Special Air Service troops from Great Britain, helped by reporting on German troop movements, attacking reinforcements and communications centers, and destroying trains and bridges. US President Dwight D. Eisenhower later said that the Resistance was like having an extra division behind enemy lines.

On August 25ᵗʰ, 1944, Free French troops led the way into Paris, where they were soon joined by Charles de Gaulle. There was still fighting in the streets, and as the six-foot-six de Gaulle marched through the streets to Notre-Dame, German snipers shot in his direction. De Gaulle did not flinch.

Illustration 56: De Gaulle and Resistance leaders marching down the Champs-Élysées with the Arc de Triomphe in the background, 8/25/1944.

French troops fought through the winter and advanced into Germany, occupying the southwestern quarter of the country as their zone of control as part of the post-war peace.

Conclusion

Charles de Gaulle presided over the French Fourth Republic from 1944 until his resignation in 1946. He left the office as he was disgusted over the infighting taking place within the political parties of France. In the vacuum left by the general, a variety of mainstream political parties, including the right, the left, and moderates, enjoyed periods of time in power. Left out of power was the extreme right, which had virtually ceased to exist after the defeat of Hitler and the betrayal of Marshal Pétain, and the radical left, which was represented by the French Communist Party, perhaps the most powerful political entity in the year or two immediately after the war.

When WWII ended, many in France wanted to see a return to the French influence and power that had existed before 1940. This was both delusional and not to be. France had been eclipsed in power by both the United States and the Soviet Union from the moment Paris fell in 1940, and the nation was never to be the same player on the international stage again.

Still, this did not stop France, with the support of the United States and Great Britain, from attempting to regain control of its former colonies. In North Africa, Algeria fell back under French control. The French zones of control in the Middle East (Lebanon and Syria) became independent nations. French colonies in Central Africa were regained only to be lost by the early 1960s, mostly bloodlessly.

Vietnam was a different story. The story is long and complicated, but suffice it to say that beginning in 1946, the French attempted to reestablish their control of the country, which began a war that increased in ferocity until 1954 with the stunning French defeat at the hands of the Vietnamese in the north at Dien Bien Phu.

In 1962, a simmering eight-year guerrilla war ended France's ownership of Algeria. The war was marked with atrocities on both sides, but the role of French troops was especially criticized at home in the light of post-war anti-imperialism and the documentation of many incidents on the new visual medium of television. The end of the war in Algeria, which was encouraged by Charles de Gaulle, who had returned to power in a bloodless sort of coup in 1958, establishing the Fifth Republic in the process, provoked ultra-nationalists in the army, specifically the elite Foreign Legion, to attempt a military coup to overthrow the government, which was put down harshly.

The 1960s were a tumultuous time for France, as they were for much of the Western world, especially the United States. In 1968, riots broke out throughout France, especially in Paris. The demonstrations and violence of 1968 in France were multi-faceted. Part of these disturbances had to do with many being opposed to America's war with Vietnam. When WWII ended, many French, having experienced German occupation, felt the reoccupation of Vietnam and Algeria was wrong. Times had changed, and the time for imperialism was over. This view was widely held, but it was primarily held by younger generations who were born just before, during, or just after WWII. Many of these people felt a kinship with the Vietnamese or somehow felt a need to atone for French involvement in the region—hence their anti-American stance. These riots also occurred because many in France felt that the WWII generation, which ruled the country, was out of touch and that it was time to move on from outdated policies and outdated thinking. Similar to the United States, the more liberal areas were urban, while the rural areas were more conservative. Also, like the USA, a culture war developed between liberals and conservatives, not only about politics but morals as well.

Internationally, the policy of de Gaulle and France after de Gaulle retired in 1969 tried to carve out an independent foreign policy. Though France was anti-communist, it also had a strong streak of anti-Americanism. This might seem odd and ungrateful to Americans, but this anti-Americanism generally did not come from a place of ingratitude, as they recognized America's part in its liberation in WWII. It came from French resentment at being replaced as a great power, American heavy-handedness and imperialism, and a desire to control its own destiny. Though most people recognized that France would support the West should a conflict develop between NATO (North Atlantic Treaty Organization) and the Soviet Union, France did not join NATO fully until 2009. It did, however, construct its own nuclear deterrent, which, though smaller than that of the US, Russia, and China, is nonetheless capable of laying waste to the entire globe.

Today, France is seen as a relatively steadfast yet sometimes critical ally of the United States, and it plays an important peace-keeping role in the world, both diplomatically and militarily. France has often sent peace-keeping forces to its former colonies in Africa and supported the US War on Terror with troops and other forces.

At home, it took many years for France to recover from WWII. Immediately after the war, it seemed to many, both in France and elsewhere, that most Frenchmen had been part of the heroic resistance movements against the Nazis, even in the parts of France controlled by French collaborationists. Between the end of the war and the late 1970s, this view changed. As you can see in the movie listed in the bibliography at the end of this book, *The Sorrow and the Pity*, many French people simply tried to get by as best they could during the war, supporting neither the Nazis nor the Resistance. It is thought that many people collaborated to one degree or another and that a smaller number actually actively resisted.

Some did both, like French President François Mitterrand (1916-1996), a power player on the international scene in the 1980s. Mitterrand's role in WWII came under intense scrutiny in his later years. It turned out that he, like many Frenchmen and women, had played both roles, collaborationist and resistor, at various times. The questions and issues (resistance versus collaboration, etc.) brought up during this time in France are still felt in the country today.

Today, France is one of the most developed nations in the world. Its current president, Emmanuel Macron, has become a world figure in his own right, claiming French leadership in the war on climate change and attempting to wrestle with serious problems in the country, especially in the areas of terrorism, immigration, minority rights, and employment issues, all of which promise to continue into the foreseeable future.

Here's another book by Captivating History
that you might like

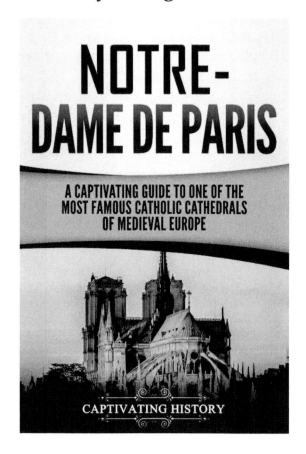

Free Bonus from Captivating History (Available for a Limited time)

Hi History Lovers!

Now you have a chance to join our exclusive history list so you can get your first history ebook for free as well as discounts and a potential to get more history books for free! Simply visit the link below to join.

Captivatinghistory.com/ebook

Also, make sure to follow us on Facebook, Twitter and Youtube by searching for Captivating History.

Appendix 1: The Fourteen Points, a simplified list of Wilson's guidelines for peace

Open covenants of peace, openly arrived at

Freedom of the seas

The removal so far as possible of all economic barriers

The reduction of national armaments to the lowest point consistent with domestic safety

Impartial adjustment of all colonial claims

The evacuation of all Russian territory

The evacuation and restoration of Belgium

The liberation of France and return of Alsace and Lorraine

Readjustment of the frontiers of Italy to conform to clearly recognizable lines of nationality

The peoples of Austria-Hungary should be accorded the freest opportunity of autonomous development

Evacuation of occupation forces from Romania, Serbia, and Montenegro; Serbia should be accorded free and secure access to the sea

Autonomous development for the non-Turkish peoples of the Ottoman Empire; free passage of the Dardanelles to the ships and commerce of all nations

An independent Poland to be established, with free and secure access to the sea

A general association of nations to be formed to guarantee to its members political independence and territorial integrity (the genesis of the League of Nations)

Bibliography

Andress, David. THE TERROR: THE MERCILESS WAR FOR FREEDOM IN REVOLUTIONARY FRANCE. London: Macmillan, 2006.

Anonymous. THE SONG OF ROLAND. North Chelmsford: Courier Corporation, 2012.

Blanning, T. C. THE NINETEENTH CENTURY: EUROPE, 1789-1914. New York: Oxford University Press, USA, 2000.

Blanning, Tim. THE PURSUIT OF GLORY: THE FIVE REVOLUTIONS THAT MADE MODERN EUROPE: 1648-1815. London: Penguin, 2007.

Bridgeford, Andrew. 1066: THE HIDDEN HISTORY IN THE BAYEUX TAPESTRY. New York: Bloomsbury Publishing USA, 2009.

Caesar, Julius. THE CONQUEST OF GAUL. London: Penguin, 1983.

"Cahiers." Accessed January 1, 2021. https://pages.uoregon.edu/dluebke/301ModernEurope/Cahiers.html.

Carey, John. EYEWITNESS TO HISTORY. New York: HarperCollins, 1997.

"Charlemagne's Travels." Wayback Machine. Accessed November 25 2020. https://web.archive.org/web/20160419073559/https://aethel raed.ddns.net/charlemagne/intro.html.

Chereau, P. (Director). (1994). QUEEN MARGOT [Dramatic retelling of the events of the St. Bartholomew's Day Massacre].

Cronk, Nicholas. VOLTAIRE: A VERY SHORT INTRODUCTION. New York: Oxford University Press, 2017.

DANTON. Directed by Andrzej Wajda. 1983. Film. (Starring Gerard Depardieu)

Davies, Peter. FRANCE AND THE SECOND WORLD WAR: OCCUPATION, COLLABORATION AND RESISTANCE. Psychology Press, 2001.

Durant, Will, and Ariel Durant. THE AGE OF LOUIS XIV: THE STORY OF CIVILIZATION. New York: Simon & Schuster, 2011.

"France Unveils Stunning Replica of Lascaux Cave Paintings." Artnet News. Last modified December 12, 2016. https://news.artnet.com/exhibitions/lascaux-cave-paintings-replica-780452.

Geary, Patrick J. READINGS IN MEDIEVAL HISTORY, *5th ed.* Toronto: University of Toronto Press, 2015.

Harrison, Kathryn. JOAN OF ARC: A LIFE TRANSFIGURED. Anchor Books, 2014.

Home · Liberty, Equality, Fraternity: Exploring the French Revolution. Accessed November 2, 2020. https://revolution.chnm.org/

Howarth, David. *1066*: THE YEAR OF THE CONQUEST. 2002.

Jackson, Julian. DE GAULLE. Cambridge: Harvard University Press, 2018.

"Jazz Liberates Paris." American Heritage. Accessed February 22, 2021. https://www.americanheritage.com/jazz-liberates-paris

Mansel, Philip. KING OF THE WORLD: THE LIFE OF LOUIS XIV. Chicago: University of Chicago Press, 2020.

"Portraits: Louis XIV." Amazon.com. Accessed December 28, 2020. https://www.amazon.com/gp/video/detail/B07CSJJQXS/ref=atv_hm_hom_1_c_iEgOEZ_2_4

Roche, Daniel. FRANCE IN THE ENLIGHTENMENT. Translated by Arthur Goldhammer. Cambridge: Harvard University Press, 1998.

Schama, Simon. CITIZENS: A CHRONICLE OF THE FRENCH REVOLUTION. Toronto: Vintage Canada, 1990.

Sebald, W.G. AUSTERLITZ. New York: Modern Library, 2011.

Simpson, Howard R. DIEN BIEN PHU: THE EPIC BATTLE AMERICA FORGOT. Lincoln: Potomac Books, 2005.

THE SORROW AND THE PITY. Directed by Marcel Ophuls. 1969. Paris, FranceFilm.

Tiersky, Ronald. FRANÇOIS MITTERRAND: A VERY FRENCH PRESIDENT. Lanham: Rowman & Littlefield, 2003.

"Treasures from Versailles – An Encounter of the Richest Kind." The Culture Concept Circle. Last modified January 13, 2017. https://www.thecultureconcept.com/treasures-from-versailles-an-encounter-of-the-richest-kind

Various. THE PORTABLE ENLIGHTENMENT READER. London: Penguin, 1995.

Wawro, Geoffrey. THE FRANCO-PRUSSIAN WAR: THE GERMAN CONQUEST OF FRANCE IN 1870-1871. Cambridge: Cambridge University Press, 2005.

Wilson, Derek. *CHARLEMAGNE*. New York: Vintage, 2007.

Printed in Great Britain
by Amazon

82202827R00149